THE
Curriculum
Mapping
PLANNER

THE

Curriculum

Mapping

PLANNER

Templates, Tools, and Resources
for Effective Professional Development

HEIDI HAYES JACOBS • ANN JOHNSON

ASCD | Alexandria, Virginia USA

1703 N. Beauregard St. • Alexandria, VA 22311-1714 USA

Phone: 800-933-2723 or 703-578-9600 • Fax: 703-575-5400

Web site: www.ascd.org • E-mail: member@ascd.org

Author guidelines: www.ascd.org/write

Gene R. Carter, *Executive Director;* Nancy Modrak, *Publisher;* Julie Houtz, *Director of Book Editing & Production;* Deborah Siegel, *Project Manager;* Greer Wymond, *Senior Graphic Designer;* Mike Kalyan, *Production Manager;* Keith Demmons, *Desktop Publishing Specialist;* Kyle Steichen, *Production Specialist*

All Web links in this book are correct as of the publication date below but may have become inactive or otherwise modified since that time. If you notice a deactivated or changed link, please e-mail books@ascd.org with the words "Link Update" in the subject line. In your message, please specify the Web link, the book title, and the page number on which the link appears.

PAPERBACK ISBN: 978-1-4166-0874-5   ASCD product #109010   n10/09

Also available as an e-book (see Books in Print for the ISBNs).

Quantity discounts for the paperback edition only: 10–49 copies, 10%; 50+ copies, 15%; for 1,000 or more copies, call 800-933-2723, ext. 5634, or 703-575-5634. For desk copies: member@ascd.org.

Library of Congress Cataloging-in-Publication Data

Jacobs, Heidi Hayes.
   The curriculum mapping planner : templates, tools, and resources for effective professional development / Heidi Hayes Jacobs and Ann Johnson.
      p. cm.
   Includes bibliographical references and index.
   ISBN 978-1-4166-0874-5
   1. Curriculum planning—Databases. 2. Curriculum evaluation—Databases. 3. School improvement programs. 4. School administrators—In-service training. I. Johnson, Ann. II. Title.
   LB2806.15.J29 2009
   375'.001—dc22
                                    2009024677

20 19 18 17 16 15 14 13 12 11 10 09   1 2 3 4 5 6 7 8 9 10 11 12

The Curriculum Mapping Planner

Templates, Tools, and Resources
for Effective Professional Development

Foreword

Building a splendid cake or an outstanding soufflé takes an inspired cook and a terrific recipe. Synchronizing an elegant dinner with multiple courses for numerous guests requires an inspired cook, terrific recipes, and alignment of complex details. Building an energized learning community takes an inspired instructional leader, a terrific recipe for facilitation, and careful alignment of what is valued with what is taught and how it is assessed.

When I was a child, my grandmother was famous for her excellent biscuits. Before I married, I watched her make them, carefully writing down each step and trying valiantly to assess how much of each ingredient she was tossing in the bowl. She rolled each pinch of dough around in her palms, patted it just so, then placed a uniformly sized circle on the sheet. I moved across the country and carefully followed the recipe I had written, trying to mimic each action step. My biscuits were not even close. When I came home a year later, the first stop was my grandmother's house so she could tell me what I did wrong.

"Let's make them together," she said. So we did. Side by side, from the same bowl, we pinched, rolled, and placed. But hers were tighter, sweeter, and more uniform.

"What is wrong with my biscuits?" I lamented.

She soothed, "Well, dear, it's all in how you handle the dough."

For years, educators have developed long range plans, pacing guides, and even detailed curriculum guides. But without laying the requisite foundation of planning, without a common knowledge with similar language, without thoughtfully guiding a process of collegial dialogue, curriculum mapping will not reach its full potential. The ingredients might be the same but the outcome is less than inspiring. The power of curriculum mapping is in teachers' dialogue about alignment so that students' learning is relevant and meaningful.

Dr. Heidi Hayes Jacobs and Dr. Ann Johnson have worked with thousands of teachers and school and district leaders over the years. Fostering a climate in which elementary teachers authentically engage in instructional dialogue with secondary level teachers requires strong instructional leadership skills. One of the most powerful pieces of the process is development of consensus maps. When teachers diary map and then come together to distill lessons into those they agree are most important, everyone has to give up some of their favorites. Facilitating discussions with teachers about what content they value most requires skill as educational leaders. This book provides the tools for instructional leaders to foster collegial dialogue and shepherd the process.

This book is a practitioner's recipe for building a community of learners, using curriculum mapping as the tool. Inspired and engaged learning is not enhanced from entering content, skills, and assessments in a template. Inspired and engaged learning is enhanced when teachers collaborate on aligned curriculum in which skills are scaffolded and competencies spiral. Leading that effort so that progress grows and sustains is a challenge that will be made much easier because of *The Curriculum Mapping Planner.* Having a map for professional development is like a recipe for "handling the dough" so that respectful collegial dialogue occurs and ultimately fosters higher levels of learning for students.

This book underscores the importance of laying the foundation for collaborative curriculum development. Schools and districts may begin in different places but the authors clearly demonstrate that "how you handle the dough" will make curriculum mapping more successful in a school or district. Having solid ingredients provided in this book and a recipe for implementation via collegial dialogue will create a higher likelihood of success in the transformational process called curriculum mapping.

Valerie Truesdale, Ph.D.
Superintendent of Beaufort County School District, South Carolina

Introduction to the Curriculum Mapping Planner

Curriculum mapping is a procedure for collecting and maintaining a database of the operational curriculum in a school or district. It provides the basis for authentic examination of the database (Jacobs, 1997). When curriculum mapping is the basis of a focused, systemic effort, it becomes a hub for connecting all aspects of the system. It serves as a linchpin, a connector, which provides the basis for

- Sharpening and focusing the curriculum to ensure a consistent core curriculum for all children.
- Connecting other school, state, and national initiatives.
- Aligning all instructional components, including content, skills, assessments, activities, and resources.
- Aligning reporting tools and processes so they provide meaningful long-term data
- Aligning all school improvement processes so they positively affect student achievement.
- Providing the data needed to develop a meaningful vision.
- Rethinking the support structure to ensure lasting change.

As educational leaders, we are constantly searching for the magic formula—the answer that would open the professional discussions that need to occur for meaningful change to take place. Curriculum mapping is a commonsense approach to address the systemic issue—improving student achievement. When it is implemented in a thoughtful manner, paying attention to everything we know about sustaining lasting change, it can have a dramatic effect on the culture of a school.

Why Map? . . . Applications

We map to solve teaching and learning problems in a specific school setting. The most common problems that mappers address have remained fundamentally the same, though the implications have evolved. We use our maps—and the review process afforded by immediate technology access—to gain information; replace repetition with spiraling classroom experiences; analyze gaps in student learning and mend them in the maps; align to standards; integrate natural curricular connections between disciplines and classrooms; update our maps on a regular basis for timeliness, given the proliferation of knowledge; and stay vigilant in our quest for internal coherence in the map.

After re-reading the following excerpt from *Mapping the Big Picture: Integrating Curriculum and Assessment K–12* (Jacobs, 1997), we are struck with how the same argument for mapping that Heidi made over a decade ago still holds:

> Though teachers may work together in the same building for years, they usually have sketchy knowledge about what goes on in each other's classrooms. High school teachers on the same corridor have no clue as to their colleagues' books, concepts, and assignments. A middle school team may work diligently on its specific program but have limited information about any other team in the building. Elementary schools can be nurturing environments but fundamentally a collection of one-room schoolhouses.

> If there are gaps among teachers within buildings, there are virtual Grand Canyons among buildings in a district. It is rare to find a high school teacher who is knowledgeable about the middle school curriculum or elementary and middle school teachers who are in close communication about their students. The reality is an occasional "transition" meeting between feeding and receiving schools where cursory information is passed on, though with the best of intentions. All too often, curriculum decisions are made in a vacuum.

> With so little real-time data available, we find two polarized tendencies. One is to become rigid and lock step with curriculum guides, giving the impression that all is under control. The second is to become so loose and vague that no one seems to have a clue as to what is going on.

> To make sense of our students' experiences over time, we need two lenses: a zoom lens into this year's curriculum for a particular grade and a wide-angle lens to see the

K–12 perspective. The classroom (or micro) level is dependent on the site and district level (a macro view).

Though the micro and macro levels are connected throughout a district, there is a conspicuous lack of macro-level data for decision making. Yet we need that big picture for each student's journey through his or her years of learning. With data from curriculum mapping, a school and its feeding and receiving sites can review and revise the curriculum within a larger, much-needed context. Data on the curriculum map can be examined both horizontally through the course of any one academic year and vertically over the student's K–12 experience.

In the past we relied on curriculum committees to provide the larger perspective. It is my contention that old-styled curriculum committees should be dismantled and replaced. Site-based curriculum councils creating curriculum maps with computers should focus on the most basic level of the students' experience in the individual school. District curriculum cabinets representing all the schools should meet periodically, taking on the role of a coordinating body akin to the editor-in-chief of a publishing house.

We need to change the process used in making curriculum decisions because most curriculum committees are ineffective at actually producing work that directly affects student performance. Curriculum committees usually come together to formulate lists of objectives, skills, and concepts that are optimum goals for teachers to implement. Occasionally these lists inspire and focus teachers' actions, but too often they remain nothing more than lifeless inventories of isolated skills. The lists may discuss 1st grade writing skills or 3rd grade reading skills, but they offer little or no focus on precisely when specific skills will be addressed during the course of a school year, let alone a group of school years.

Without a commitment to when a skill will be taught, there is no commitment. Furthermore, skills are not taught in a vacuum. They are addressed in application to content, and they are evidenced in a product or performance by the learner. In short, though committees anguish over the skill list, most end up with the feeling that it is not a useful document. As one teacher put it, "There is a sense of let's get through this, because they're making us." District-level educators become all the more frustrated when the skill list is filed away, and no one really knows if and how the skills are used.

No teacher or administrator is to blame for this situation. None of us chooses to make the absence of efficient or effective communication a reality. It has long been difficult to find out or plan curriculum within a broader context. Teachers cannot run up and down the halls of their buildings with notepads gathering information about curriculum and assessment. They cannot call every teacher each student has had for the past few years. Constant meetings outside school hours are ineffective and expensive.

We need a 21st century approach. Curriculum mapping amplifies the possibilities for long-range planning, short-term preparation, and clear communication.

Our students need us to know their experiences over the course of time. They need us to know what's really going on in their daily classes as they move among teachers and subjects. They need us to know and give credence to their work from year to year. With that information, possibilities emerge. (pp. 3–5)

Background on Curriculum Mapping... and Our Collaboration

The seeds of Heidi Hayes Jacobs' curriculum mapping model come from several sources. One influence was the early work of Fenwick English (1992) on curriculum audits. His notion was *monitor content mapping*. In this approach, a third party would attempt to objectively review whether targeted content topics were addressed through the course of a school year. A key turning point for Heidi came from her doctoral studies at Columbia University Teachers College in the late 1970s on the nature of integrated curriculum and epistemology. She began to see that most of these efforts were "unit" design based, and as she began to work in schools through the 1980s, it was clear that there was a hunger for the big picture K–12.

Upon receiving her degree, Heidi went on to serve as an adjunct associate professor at Teachers College during the 1980s and 1990s when the Writing Project, under the leadership of Dr. Lucy Caulkins, began to expand exponentially across the country. Heidi's interaction with Dr. Caulkins and many of her colleagues prompted a rethinking of the "curriculum writing process" as well. The notion of drafts, revision, voice, and publishing curriculum work emerged in her thinking and writing. Concurrently, there was the emergence of the Internet and new technologies. A classroom teacher from the Westport, Connecticut, schools, Werner Liepolt, approached Heidi in the early 1990s with the idea that curriculum mapping could eventually be shifted to a software-based program. He was the first pioneer in what is now global sharing of curriculum mapping. With years of consulting and field work in schools across the nation, the seven-step model was refined and eventually published by ASCD. Key education technology leaders responded with software that has added dimensions to the work throughout the world.

A turning point in refining the model occurred in the mid 1990s when Heidi began to field-test a seven-stage model in school districts. There were two administrators who wanted to implement the model in their respective schools with great courage and enthusiasm. At an

ASCD conference held in Colorado, Heidi was approached by Dr. Ann Johnson, who was working in Iowa with the Ankeny School District. The other leader was Mary Ann Holt, who was serving as an elementary principal in Chattanooga, Tennessee. Ann and Mary Ann "got mapping" from the beginning and believed it had the potential to improve communication and ultimately learning in their respective schools. Each of these visionaries has been featured in publications and DVD programs developed by ASCD. Both of these practitioners felt that a training manual needed to eventually emerge that could provide direction and help to their colleagues.

This training manual is intended to provide leaders with a map to guide professional development as they work to implement curriculum mapping in their school. It is not intended to be the answer, but it is intended to help them focus on the key components that are essential to ensure successful implementation.

Becoming a Curriculum Mapping Learning Organization

Curriculum mapping can be applied to any educative endeavor, including professional development. With this in mind, we have created a four-phase professional development program composed of 12 modules, which are presented as 12 curriculum maps. In short, this book will help you map "mapping." Our sincere hope is to provide some guidance to the many staff developers, teacher leaders, administrators, regional service centers, and national educators concerned with moving their constituents into a 21st century approach to creating curriculum.

Moving into mapping requires a genuine paradigm shift. Rather than filing curriculum guides on shelves in binders, educators throughout the world share their work electronically. With immediate access to their work, classroom teachers can indicate precisely what curriculum they have been able to share with their specific learners, what skills and strategies are being nurtured, and conversely which ones need ongoing attention. Assessments can be reviewed openly, both vertically K–12 and across grade levels, with an eye to diagnosing student needs.

The trends in mapping are dynamic, reflecting the power of the technology tools we use to share our work. The new import/export business in education is the uploading and downloading of curriculum maps nationally and internationally between classroom teachers. With the advent of digital portfolios, we are seeing students mapping as they link their personal work samples to their teachers' curriculum maps.

These exciting outcomes are possible when a school or other education organization makes the successful transition to a professional learning community that maps. This manual is designed to assist you in making that transition. Appreciating the genuine demands that this work requires, we have laid out the work in an organized four-phase approach composed of incrementally designed modules reflecting the mapping process itself.

The Four Phases for Curriculum Mapping Professional Development are as follows:

- Laying the Foundation
- Launching the Process
- Maintaining, Sustaining, and Integrating the System
- Advanced Mapping Tasks

In our own collaboration while preparing this work, we reflected on the many situations in both public and independent school environments where a surprising adaptation needed to be made. No two schools are alike. Some of you reading this manual have a highly diverse student population with many English language learners. Some of you have a "batch" of first-year teachers. Some of you have small classes filled with high-performing students under enormous pressure to achieve. Some of you have difficult staff relations between teachers and administration. The list does, indeed, go on. We recognize that range, and we understand that you will be making adaptations to our recommendations. To support you in your efforts, here are a few baseline assumptions that we support and ask you to consider as you begin to design and implement a mapping plan.

Differentiated Staff Development is key to successful professional development (Jacobs, 2006). One-size-fits-all does not work when educating adults. As you read through the modules and review our proposed maps, we suggest that you identify how you might best set up specific grouping patterns with corresponding venues to assist your colleagues. Whether it is one teacher sitting with another at a laptop computer, a small group at a work session examining maps, an online course for an individual teacher, a regional workshop, or a video conference with another school involved with mapping, we encourage you to avoid the reflexive pattern of always going straight to the workshop approach.

Differentiated Building Development is equally important. In school districts where there are many buildings, it is easy for central office to "demand" that everyone meet targets in a plan identically. It is almost a pacing-guide approach to staff development, and it will certainly be unsuccessful. We advocate a sensible recognition that buildings have unique cultures, different constituents, and different faculty members. This is not to say that there should not be common targets; rather, we are saying that given the transition from 20th to 21st century practices for building, sharing, reviewing, and updating curriculum, schools need to move at a pace and with an approach that will work. Pragmatism is critical to long-term growth.

Technology is Central to Mapping. The old paper-and-pencil approach, and even the word-processing-document model, are counterproductive. By their very nature, these old approaches limit access. They privatize curriculum as opposed to fostering open sharing between members of a professional community. Today, mapping software allows for immediate revision and adjustments in real time. And, most important, it provides the remarkable and modern capacity for immediate sharing between specific educators with shared concerns, whether it is a middle school social studies teacher examining an elementary history map or a high school teacher in Australia interacting with mathematics teachers and their maps from Toronto, Canada, and Atlanta, Georgia, regarding an approach to algebra.

We wish to acknowledge the extraordinary contribution of the mapping software developers who make the work possible. They add tremendous insight and expand the possibilities. We wish to acknowledge one of the not-for-profit programs developed by the GST BOCES of New York called Mapster for their easy-to-follow tutorials, and their modeling of the important role of regional service centers in supporting systemic initiatives. There are local school districts that developed sophisticated software solutions as exemplified by the David Douglas District in the greater Portland, Oregon, area. There, school leaders and technology gurus created a powerful tool to assist mapping work. There are several commercial software groups that we believe have created remarkably facile and dynamic programs. Because of their work, their teams, and their innovations, mapping is now global.

The programs are

- Atlas Curriculum Management System: www.rubiconatlas.com/mapping.htm
- The Curriculum Mapper: www.clihome.com/curriculummapper
- Curricuplan: www.curricuplan.com
- Performance Pathways: www.techpaths.com
- School Software Group: www.schoolsoftwaregroup.com

We do not advocate any one program, commercial or not-for-profit, but we do feel strongly that using a software vendor is critical to the long-term success of your efforts. The key to making the connections between your hardworking educators within buildings, across schools, and around the world employing excellent software will be thorough and thoughtful professional development reflecting the principles of curriculum mapping design. We encourage your examination of the four phases and their inherent modules to assist you in your efforts.

How to Use the Curriculum Mapping Planner

This training manual was designed to serve as an instructional map for leaders and leadership teams to guide them in developing quality training for their teachers and administrators in the process of curriculum mapping. The training maps included in the modules include the critical components to provide a solid foundation in curriculum mapping and set the stage for lasting change. This manual is a companion to the range of the identified books in our resource section at the end of each module.

Your R and D Team

It has been our experience that successful mapping initiatives start with a leadership cadre at each building (Jacobs, 2004). This advanced guard begins the R&D process of researching the mapping process through reading, conferences, interviews, site visits, and online courses. They are the key players who are the first users of the manual you hold in your hands. Mapping is generally most effective when it commences at the building level with a small number of teacher leaders and at least one administrator beginning the study group. Their work will allow them to develop the very professional development map we encourage in the manual. We encourage you to take the time you need to get ready to make what will ultimately be a move into the 21st century that will replace old ways of storing curricula in binders on shelves. Your team will do well to have a range of viewpoints represented, with at least one member who is "tech savvy."

The Layout of the Manual

The Curriculum Mapping Planner is divided into four sections that represent major phases in the implementation of the curriculum mapping process: Laying the Foundation; Launching the Process; Maintaining, Sustaining, and Integrating the System; and Advanced Mapping Tasks. Within each section are specific training modules that include instructional maps. These modules can be used by leadership teams to develop high-quality training to coach their school or district through the mapping process. Each of the 12 modules begins with an overview of the module that explains the purpose for the module and why the content is critical to a deeper understanding of curriculum mapping.

Twelve Professional Development Maps

Each module has been converted into a professional development map. Not only does this give you a clear and useful blueprint to guide your planning, but it models the nature of curriculum mapping itself. The professional development map contains essential questions that provide a focus for training, suggested concepts and content to be taught, skills that participants should be able to demonstrate following the training, and assessment(s) or evidence of learning to be produced during the training session(s). In addition, the maps contain the following items.

The Activities, Supporting Materials, and Time Frame

A wide variety of sample activities that provide practice experiences so the participants can successfully demonstrate the identified skills are included in professional development maps. In addition to the suggested activities, the map also describes the materials that will be needed to successfully complete the activities and a suggested time frame for the activities. The activities can easily be tailored or adjusted to fit the needs of the participants based upon their background and knowledge in this area. Additional materials for each module can be found online.

Assignments and Resources

As part of each professional development map, we have included possible follow-up assignments and resources. The assignments can provide follow-up practice for the participants, help them maintain focus on curriculum mapping, and help set the stage and prepare them for the next training. The resources provide additional information and can be used in study groups or as a support to the activities.

Tips and Suggestions for Using the Manual

We would encourage school or district leadership teams to work collaboratively through the modules to gain a shared understanding of curriculum mapping and how it might look in their school or district. A school or district might use this as the cornerstone for a study group session the year prior to implementation. Potential leaders from across the school or district could be invited to participate. This would allow a school or district to broaden its leadership structure to ensure a solid support base when it is rolled out within a school or a district. As the study group team works through the process, we would encourage you to discuss each module and identify any possible changes or additions you might want to make to tailor it for your staff.

Your Own Professional Development Maps

Obviously, the goal is for you to adapt and apply these modules for your own local needs. We believe the best practice will be to begin to draft your own professional development maps either on your existing software (if you are currently mapping) or on a word processing document if you are currently considering choosing your software solution. We encourage you to start mapping.

I.

Laying the
FOUNDATION

Prologue for the Planners:
Getting the Basics

"Prologue" in Greek means "before the action of the play." Setting the stage, literally and figuratively, elevates the attention of all participants (Jacobs, 2004). Perhaps one of the greatest indicators of success is the thoughtful planning that takes place before actual implementation begins. Schools and districts across the country that have experienced success with the curriculum mapping process have taken time in the beginning to "lay the foundation" needed for lasting change. All have taken the time to gain a deeper understanding of mapping and used this information to develop a comprehensive plan to ensure successful implementation. Some schools have formed study groups and worked with a small group of teacher leaders to gain a deeper understanding before launching the mapping process schoolwide. Other schools have sent representatives to conferences and then worked collaboratively to bring the information back to their schools or districts. Still others have used samples from other schools and districts to begin the discussion in their own school. Schools who do not establish a solid foundation for mapping struggle to sustain long-term change.

Curriculum mapping is a procedure for collecting and maintaining a database of the operational curriculum in a school or district. It provides the vehicle to authentically examine the curriculum and its relationship to other aspects of the system. For this reason, curriculum mapping is far more than the development of individual or schoolwide maps. It is a hub for all school improvement efforts in the school or district. Schools who have implemented curriculum mapping from a systemic perspective find it leads to a more dynamic, focused curriculum; stronger alignment with assessments, instructions, and reporting; new ways of collecting and analyzing data; a more cohesive approach to planning and implementing professional development; and an opportunity to strengthen the organizational and leadership structure in a school or district.

After working to implement curriculum mapping using a systemic approach, one school's leadership team received the following feedback from staff when asked about the impact curriculum mapping had had on their school. Staff members said it provided

- A guaranteed, nonnegotiable curriculum for all students in all grades and subjects.
- A sharper focus and alignment in curriculum, instruction, assessment, and professional development.
- Alignment of instruction to the content standards and benchmarks in all content areas, plus increased accountability for instruction.
- Access to meaningful data about instruction, assessment, and student learning.
- A vehicle for integration of critical cross-curricular skills.
- An increased awareness of the research-based link between teaching and learning.
- A greater awareness of what other teachers in the department, team, or grade level were teaching.
- More professional discussions regarding teaching and learning because of the curriculum maps.
- A clearer sense of vision and how "the pieces fit together" (e.g., curriculum, assessment, instruction, professional development, data, and reporting).

When curriculum mapping is implemented using a thoughtful, systemic approach, most schools or districts will have this type of experience. The time invested in developing the plan and bringing staff onboard will provide the strong foundation needed to sustain your efforts when you encounter "bumps along the way." It is a journey that can strengthen and enhance an instructional program and have a dramatic impact on student achievement.

Purpose and Primary Focus

This module is targeted for you, the planners and leadership cadre responsible for molding a plan for mapping in your school or district. The activities included in this module have been structured so they explore these key questions: What is curriculum mapping? How can curriculum mapping influence student achievement? How can curriculum mapping serve as a lens or filter to sharpen teaching and learning in your school or district? In addition to having the opportunity to gain a basic understanding of curriculum mapping, leaders and teams will also participate in activities that they can use, modify, or expand with their own staffs.

Types of Maps

In the last few years, when introducing the mapping concept to teachers we have used the analogy of MapQuest. It is an apt example, because the user of MapQuest can get the level of detail needed to match a task. If I need driving directions, I can easily get highly specific road maps that will take me from Times Square in New York City to the steps of the statehouse in Harrisburg, Pennsylvania. But, sometimes that is too much detail and can actually conflict with the task. If I need to see where Harrisburg is located in relationship to Philadelphia and Pittsburgh, then I need to go to a wider angle and get a state map or perhaps a map of the Mid-Atlantic States. In short, the beauty of the technology is that location and direction can be handled with ease on MapQuest. In a similar way, using curriculum mapping technology allows educators to access the level of detail they need in order to address certain tasks. There are, in short, different types of maps for different types of functions. Becoming familiar with the different types of maps is critical for the planning teams.

The individual classroom teacher's curriculum map. This map conveys the operational curriculum based on the actual school calendar. It is a clear and useful summary that can easily be understood and read by colleagues within and between buildings in a school or district.

Consensus maps. These maps are less detailed than the classroom teacher's map because their function is not to reflect the operational curriculum but rather to project agreed-upon areas of focus for a school or district. Through the consensus review process, not only are the requisite content, skill, assessment, and essential questions for all students in a district identified but also those areas where flexibility is appropriate. For example, there might be an agreement that all 4th grade teachers will introduce historical fiction, but there will be flexibility as to the choice of books. The classroom teacher's map will show what those choices are for each 4th grade teacher.

There are a number of different names used for consensus maps: essential map, district map, core maps, and master maps. It is our view that any of these will suffice, but it is important that all members of your school or district use the same names for their maps. Module 7 focuses on developing consensus maps.

Elements on the Map

All compositions have elements. Composers make choices about the elements, then fuse them to make a coherent composition. Whether it is a writer with "characters, plot, and setting" or a musical composer with "melody, harmony, and rhythm" or an architect with "style, materials, and proportion," composers attempt to select those elements that work together effectively. Teachers make choices for their curricular compositions in their selection of content, skills, and assessments. With mapping, we have an opportunity to make these choices both within our classrooms and in sync both vertically and horizontally. Embraced by a set of essential questions, the curriculum map becomes a living document designed to match the needs of specific learners. This module will ask you to become clear about the nature of these elements in order to build school capacity for ongoing review and revision of our work. If the elements are not clear, then communication between colleagues becomes confusing and hinders progress.

Activities and Supporting Materials

Activities included in this module will help staff to clarify the definition of curriculum mapping by examining what it is and what it isn't through a study group activity, a workshop, small group activities, discussions, team exercises, and large group activities.

The curriculum maps provided for use in the sample map activities are in various stages of design. Some are beginning maps and others represent maps that have gone through several revisions. The selection was purposeful to encourage participants to think about what constitutes quality maps. What is the purpose of a map? What information should be included on a map? How detailed should the map be?

Content, concepts, "Big Ideas," essential questions, guiding questions, benchmark skills, critical skills, grade-level expectations, and objectives are all examples of terms used in schools and districts nationwide. Every school or district may define and use these terms differently. What may be a critical skill in one school may be called a benchmark skill in another. For obvious reasons, the terminology used can cause major confusion in a school or district in the beginning stages. To avoid this problem, it is important to reach consensus on a common glossary of terms for your district or school. These important decisions, if made early in the process, can help avoid needless confusion and problems later as you work to implement curriculum mapping schoolwide. To provide further support to their staffs, some schools have found it helpful to develop a glossary of terms to help staff in the initial stages of mapping. This can be an invaluable support tool to staffs as they become more confident with the terminology and the mapping process. Some schools have gone so far as to link them to their Web sites so both staff and parents have access to them. The activity on Making Sense of the Old and New Terms in this module sets the stage for beginning this discussion in your school or district.

Training Tips

The activities suggested in this training module may be completed all in the same session if time permits or may be completed in separate sessions. Some schools opt to start with the study group activity and readings from identified books, and then hold sessions before or after school to use the other activities to help reinforce the information gleaned in the slides and readings. Activities included in this outline may be modified or adjusted to accommodate the size of the group. Information in this module may also be taught in conjunction with Module 2. Coupled with the activities in Module 2, the information and activities included in Module 1 can provide the deep understanding needed to implement curriculum mapping successfully in your school or district. We recommend you begin to map your own school's or district's implementation plan as soon as possible (see Module 10, Developing a Professional Development/Implementation Plan).

Please avoid the temptation to cut short this module. Schools or districts who have done so have found increased challenges later in the implementation process. "Laying the Foundation" is a critical first step in the implementation process. Because of the systemic nature of the process, it is important to take the time to help a staff gain a strong foundational understanding of the concept and how it can serve as a connector for all aspects of the system.

To sustain lasting change, the old adage "Go slow to go fast" has merit when laying a solid foundation in the process of curriculum mapping.

Online Materials

To use this module, you'll need to access the following online documents:

Module 1, Figure 1: Definition of Curriculum Mapping

Module 1, Figure 2: Two Sides of a Coin

Module 1, Figure 3: Making Sense of the Terms (Sample)

Module 1, Figure 4: Elements of Curriculum Maps

Module 1, Figure 5: 1st Grade Math Curriculum Map

Module 1, Figure 6: 2nd Grade Geography Curriculum Map

Module 1, Figure 7: 5th Grade Math Curriculum Map

Module 1, Figure 8: 7th Grade Science Curriculum Map

Module 1, Figure 9: 8th Grade Writing Curriculum Map

Module 1, Figure 10: 10th Grade Biology Curriculum Map

Module 1, Figure 11: 10th Grade Chemistry Curriculum Map

Module 1, Figure 12: 10th Grade Poetry Curriculum Map

Module 1, Figure 13: Deaf Education Curriculum Map

Online Access

All of the figures are available for download at **www.ascd.org/downloads.**

Enter this unique key to unlock the files: **G99A3-075ED-04D1A**

If you have difficulty accessing the files, e-mail webhelp@ascd.org or call
1-800-933-ASCD for assistance.

ESSENTIAL QUESTIONS

- Curriculum mapping: What is it?
- How can curriculum mapping impact student learning?
- How can curriculum mapping serve as a lens or filter to sharpen teaching and learning in your school or district?

CONTENT

Concept: Curriculum mapping is a systematic process for ongoing curriculum and assessment review.

- Definition of Curriculum Mapping
- Two Sides of a Coin: The Maps and the Review Process
- Current State of Mapping in the Country and Worldwide Use
- Purpose and Rationale: The Problems Mapping Addresses
- MAPPING IS A VERB: The Seven-Stage Curriculum Mapping Review Model
- Types of Maps and Their Functions
- ELEMENTS on a Map
- Terminology: Making Sense of the Terms
- Products Produced through the Curriculum Mapping Process
- **TERMS** "Big Ideas," Consensus Maps, Curriculum Mapping, Diary Maps, Enduring Understandings, Individual Maps, Projection Maps

SKILLS

- Determine what curriculum mapping is and isn't.
- Describe the relationship between the "two sides of the coin" and what happens if one or the other is missing.
- Explain the reasons for the widespread use of mapping.
- Brainstorm problems or issues in your school or district that could be addressed with curriculum mapping.
- Summarize each of the seven steps of the review cycle and explain the purpose of each phase.
- Review sample maps to determine consistent elements, possible information that can be gleaned from maps, and possible uses.
- Distinguish between old and new curriculum terms.
- Identify possible products and end results that could be generated by implementing the curriculum mapping process.

EVIDENCE OF LEARNING

- Team summary notes from the Overview Session (i.e., definition, ah hahs, questions, what mapping is and isn't)
- Visual description of the two-sided coin
- Reasons for widespread use of mapping
- List of problems and issues to be addressed
- Metaphor or analogy summarizing the Seven-Step Review Model
- Team summary of consistent elements, information gleaned, and possible uses
- Graphic organizer distinguishing between the old and new terms
- List of possible products from the mapping process

ACTIVITIES

Laying the Foundation (study group)
Read Chapters 1 and 2 in *Mapping the Big Picture* or Chapters 1 and 3 in *Keys to Curriculum Mapping*. These chapters could be assigned ahead of time, be jig-sawed during the training session, or read following the first session to provide more background. As a team, generate a list of key points and questions to be addressed.

Overview of Curriculum Mapping (workshop)
Use the information gleaned from the chapters read in the first activity to provide an overview and a "big picture" perspective. In small groups, determine what mapping is and isn't, share ah-hahs, and identify questions the group may have regarding curriculum mapping.

Two-Sided Coin (small group exercise)
- Use the coin hand-out provided in the materials as a guide and in small groups, draw both sides of a coin on chart paper that visually represents its connection with mapping. What could you include on each side of the coin that shows the connections with mapping?
- Discuss what happens if one side is missing.
- Share your group's representation with the other groups.
- As a team process, what became clearer as you worked on this activity?

Why Mapping? (discussion)
- Consider the information in Chapters 1 and 2 in *Mapping the Big Picture*. At your table, discuss why curriculum mapping has gained momentum.
- Share your main reasons in the larger group.

Problems and Issues (team brainstorming exercise)
- In school or district teams, brainstorm problems or issues in your school or district that could be addressed through the mapping process.
- Share your list with others at your table.

The Seven-Step Review Model (small-group exercise)
- In small groups, create a metaphor or analogy to summarize the important points in the Seven-Step Review Model. (See pages 8–16 of *Mapping the Big Picture*.)
- Share your metaphor or analogy with the other groups.
- Discuss in the large group the importance of the Seven-Step Review Model to the mapping process.

Sample Maps (individual and group exercise)
- Use a packet of sample maps from different grade levels and subjects provided in the training module, and individually select a few from the packet and study them in more depth.
- Note consistent elements that occur on all maps, types of information gleaned from the maps, and quality elements (i.e., elements on specific maps that seem to be better or provide more information than others).
- After 10–15 minutes, in small groups reach consensus on the elements, information that can be gleaned from maps, and possible uses.

- As a group, be prepared to report out to the larger group. The facilitator may find it helpful to capture some of this information.

Making Sense of Old and New Terms (table team exercise)
- Have participants at each table write terms with a marker on half sheets of paper that are used with the current curriculum.
- Then, write down new terms used in curriculum mapping. (You may wish to use different colors of paper for the old and new terms.)
- After table teams have generated a list of terminology used with the current curriculum and with curriculum mapping, have the participants lay the half sheets out on the table or tape them to the wall.
- On the left-hand side put the terminology used with the current curriculum process.
- On the right-hand side lay out the terminology used with curriculum mapping. Match the terms on the left side with terms identified for curriculum mapping. Discuss synonyms, terms that take the place of the previous terms, etc.
- Combine with another table team and bring the two lists together.
- In the large group, discuss how this activity could be used with school or district staffs when there is confusion regarding the terms.
- A collection template is provided for this activity in the supporting materials.

Possible Products/End Results (team exercise)
- In your table teams, generate a list of possible products or end results that could be produced in the curriculum mapping process.
- Share your list in the large group setting.

ASSIGNMENTS

- Individually brainstorm a list of what you believe are strengths in your school or district's current curriculum and a list of changes that if made in the current curriculum might have a greater effect on improved student performance. Bring the list to the next training session.
- Individually brainstorm a list of the current initiatives in your building and bring them to the next training session.
- Bring a copy of the school or district achievement data to the next training session.

RESOURCES

Hale, J. (2007). *A Guide to Curriculum Mapping*. Thousand Oaks, CA: Corwin Press. Chapters 2, 3, and 4.

Jacobs, H.H. (1997). *Mapping the Big Picture: Integrating Curriculum and Assessment K–12*. Alexandria, VA: ASCD. Chapters 1–2.

Jacobs, H.H. (2004). *Getting Results with Curriculum Mapping*. Alexandria, VA: ASCD. Chapters 1–2.

Jacobs, H.H. (2007). Resources on Web site—www.curriculumdesigners.com

Jacobs, H.H. (in press). *Curriculum 21: Essential Education for a Changing World*. Alexandria, VA: ASCD.

Udelhofen, S. (2005). *Keys to Curriculum Mapping: Strategies and Tools to Make It Work*. Thousand Oaks, CA: Corwin Press. Chapters 1–3.

Establishing Your School's or District's Reason to Map

"Establishing Your School's or District's Reason to Map" is an important motivator to help anchor change and sustain it long term. We map to solve problems. Two fundamental and universal reasons for mapping are integrating assessment findings directly into our maps, and using curriculum mapping software to become the hub for housing initiatives.

In *Mapping the Big Picture*, Jacobs (1997) first established fundamental tasks that school personnel used to identify the problems they wished to attack. These tasks were noted in Module 1—gaining information, eliminating redundancies, analyzing gaps, validating standards, integrating curricula, updating for timeliness, and aligning for coherence. Selecting one of these tasks and making an adaptation that is needed in your school setting is the heart of establishing purpose.

We believe that a core reason to map is to view assessment data from our learners as the basis of diagnosis and the revision of curriculum maps as the basis of a responsive prescription. Medical doctors run tests on us when we have symptoms of discomfort and make a diagnosis as to the cause of the problem based on testing. With that information, they can give us a prescription to make the necessary changes for improvement. In our schools, we assess our students' performance to make a diagnosis and respond with prescriptive revisions and changes in our maps.

Certainly, one of the most helpful strategies involves the analysis of achievement data. Through the analysis of achievement data and other data in a system, a school or district can underscore the need for change. By actively involving staff in the process, mapping helps to create buy in by working collaboratively to identify the strengths and targets for growth.

Together, you are able to assess what's working and what is not. Assessment data from this analysis can provide a valuable hook or entry point into the mapping process by identifying the targeted areas that need to be addressed. This self-assessment phase can help "lay the foundation" for mapping in a school or district.

Fragmentation is running rampant in our schools. Teachers find themselves drowning in a sea of initiatives. They often are implemented in isolation and teachers struggle to determine what is most important and how to manage everything. Mapping becomes a connector. If the connections are not made, mapping becomes just one more thing to do or "juggle." By creating a visual connection with the staff to show how mapping serves as a vehicle to help manage and integrate the other initiatives, it can help provide momentum for initiating the mapping process. It also can help lower anxiety and help sustain the work in other initiatives.

Setting the stage in your school or district is a critical step in the process. If staff has a clear understanding of the reasons for mapping, it helps provide the anchor needed to ensure lasting, long-term change.

Purpose and Primary Focus

Module 2 is structured to help participants establish the reasons for mapping in their school or district by identifying possible obstacles to mapping and considering possible entry or starting points in the process. Guiding questions that provide focus for this module include: So why should we map? How can we determine our school or district's readiness status? What does the school value and feel are its current strengths as it relates to curriculum? What changes, if made in the current curriculum, could strengthen it so it could have a greater impact on student performance? How could curriculum mapping serve as a vehicle to help make those changes? How does mapping connect with other initiatives currently being implemented in the school or district? and What are possible entry points into the mapping process?

Activities and Supporting Materials

To help provide a rich background for "Establishing Your School's or District's Reason to Map," we have provided a variety of activities to engage the participants in the learning process. Included are team exercises, data analysis exercises, brainstorming exercises, discussions, and small and large group work.

Participants begin by considering both future trends and the strengths and weaknesses of their current curriculum, and then move into analyzing data to validate strengths in achievement and identify targets for growth. If a school or district's achievement data are aligned to the critical skill sets, it can be a powerful tool in determining gaps and redundancies in the curriculum. Schoolwide data provide a snapshot that can be helpful in gaining a more complete picture of learning in the system. The examination of data can also affirm the need for a focused process to align all components of the system. Problems arise when the data are vague or do not align with the actual curriculum in a school. Although this experience can be frustrating too, the fact that the data are not aligned to the grade-level expectations is data in itself.

Many schools or districts are so immersed in initiatives that introducing curriculum mapping can sometimes leave the staff feeling even more anxious if there isn't a strategy in place to address their concerns. Curriculum mapping becomes "just one more thing that has to be done" or is inflicted upon them. Mapping the current initiatives in a building or district can be a helpful tool in gaining a better understanding of the magnitude of change that is currently taking place in the system. The information gleaned from mapping the initiatives and identifying the "value-added" can be used as a visual to show staff how curriculum mapping can be a hub to connect all aspects of the school improvement. It also can strengthen the case for implementing curriculum mapping.

By assessing the status of the school or district, you can glean valuable data allowing you to tailor the implementation of curriculum mapping to better meet the needs of your school or district. Thus curriculum mapping becomes a "valued-added" process instead of just another initiative invading your stakeholders' professional lives. By maintaining a "value-added" focus, you minimize the number of times you hear the age-old question: So why are we doing this?

Another common question that is frequently asked by staffs when a new initiative is undertaken in a school or district is: So where are we going with this? The fear underlying this question is the concern that what they have been doing previously is wrong. The "From…To" activity, developed by Bena Kallick, in this section can support the work that has been done previously in a school or district and can also help teachers think about how curriculum mapping can enhance the work as it relates to curriculum, instruction, assessment, professional development, and other aspects of school improvement. It also can help to ease concerns, particularly for veteran staff, by visually helping staff to see how curriculum mapping is an evolution and enhancement of previous work in those areas.

Training Tips

The activities suggested in this training module may be completed in the same session if time permits or may be completed in separate sessions. The activities may also be completed in conjunction with the training Module 1. Some leadership teams have opted to combine the two modules because they so closely support each other.

A question that is sometimes asked is: Should the assessment of the school's current status precede an introduction to curriculum mapping? To address this question, it is important that you know your staff so you can determine which would be the most effective entry point to begin to develop a case for implementing curriculum mapping.

Online Materials

To use this module, you'll need to access the following online documents:

Module 2, Figure 1: Strengths and Changes

Module 2, Figure 2: Data Analysis: Steps to consider

Module 2, Figure 3: Data Analysis Questions

Module 2, Figure 4: Puzzle Pieces Template

Module 2, Figure 5: Implementation Entry Points

Module 2, Figure 6: Entry Points Graphic Organizer

Module 2, Figure 7: Obstacles and Solutions

Module 2, Figure 8: From. . . To. . . Sample

Module 2, Figure 9: From. . . To. . . Template

ESSENTIAL QUESTIONS

- So why map?
- How can you determine your school or district's current readiness status?
- What are possible entry points to mapping?

CONTENT

Concept: Establishing the reasons to map in your school or district can lay the foundation for lasting change.

- Strengths and Limitations of the Current Curriculum in Your School or District
- Analysis of Assessment Data
- Current School Improvement Initiatives
- Entry Points to the Mapping Process
- Reasons to Map
- From . . . To
- Curriculum Mapping as a Hub
- **TERMS** Data Analysis, Entry Points, Hub Skills

SKILLS

- Identify strengths in the current curriculum and changes that would positively impact student achievement.
- Analyze school or district data to determine strengths and targets for growth.
- Connect other school or district initiatives to the curriculum mapping process.
- Identify possible entry points for the mapping process.
- Summarize the reasons for your school or district to map.
- Brainstorm possible obstacles to mapping and generate possible solutions to address those obstacles.
- Explain the evolution of curriculum, assessment, instruction, and professional development in your school or district.
- Predict how curriculum mapping could serve as a hub for school improvement.

EVIDENCE OF LEARNING

- List of strengths and changes that would enhance the curriculum generated by the group
- List of strengths and targets for growth identified by the data teams using the puzzle pieces
- Graphic organizer that identifies possible entry points for implementing curriculum mapping
- List of reasons for your school or district to map
- List of obstacles and possible solutions
- Graphic organizer "From . . . To" (depicting the evolution of curriculum, assessment, instruction, and PD in your school)
- Curriculum mapping as a hub organizer used to identify possible entry points for the integration of curriculum mapping

ACTIVITIES

Thinking about the Future (small group exercise)

- In small groups, brainstorm five or six innovations, inventions, discoveries, or technological advancements that have occurred during the past five years that have had or will have an impact on the curriculum.

- Discuss the potential impact on the curriculum. What changes will need to be made?
- As a team, brainstorm what skills will be critical for students in the future.
- Discuss whether or not they are being addressed in the current curriculum.
- Be prepared to share an advancement and sample skills in the large group.

Strengths and Limitations (small group exercise)

- In small groups, brainstorm the current curriculum and write them on the left column of a piece of chart paper.
- Then, ask the teams to identify possible changes that if made would strengthen the curriculum for students and better prepare them for the future. Write these in the right column.
- Post all sheets in the front of the room and note similarities.
- Discuss how mapping could help to address some of the changes.

Data Teams (data analysis team exercise)

- In school teams, examine the assessment data for your school or district. You may want to look at all of the data or you may want to narrow your focus to one specific area such as reading or math. What data would give you the best picture of student performance in your school or district?
- As a data team, identify the strengths and targets for growth.
- Identify additional information that would help you have a more complete picture of learning.
- Share your findings with other teams.
- Discuss how mapping could help you address the deficit areas.

Connecting Initiatives (team exercise)

- Ask teams to brainstorm a list of current building or district initiatives. Write each initiative on one of the puzzle pieces provided.
- Then, brainstorm the value added for students by implementing that initiative and add those as bullet points under the initiative.
- After the team has completed this process for all initiatives, ask them to lay the pieces out on the table and discuss the common themes that surface.
- Next, write the term "curriculum mapping" in the center of one of the blank puzzle pieces.
- List the value added to students as bullet points under curriculum mapping.
- As a team, discuss the connections.

Identifying the Entry Points (team exercise)

- Use the graphic organizer provided in this module to map possible entry or starting points for curriculum mapping.
- Write curriculum mapping in the center oval.
- Ask the team to brainstorm possible processes or projects in which the school or district is engaged and write them on the spokes.
- Discuss possible links between curriculum mapping and these projects, processes, or initiatives. How could mapping be integrated as you continue to work in these areas?

Reasons to Map (group exercise)

- Generate a list of reasons why your schools and districts should map. What problems could mapping address?

Obstacles and Opportunities (small group exercise)

- In small groups, draw a T chart on chart paper that has been provided. Brainstorm a list of potential obstacles you will need to overcome in your school or district. Place the potential obstacles on the left side.
- On the right side, generate possible solutions.
- Share highlights in the large group.

From . . . To Visual Summary (team exercise)

- In the early part of the implementation process, it is helpful to develop a visual or graphic that identifies the critical components such as curriculum, assessment, instruction, and professional development and ask staff to think about how each has evolved over the past few years. (A visual is provided in the online materials.)
- In your school or district teams, write the words, "curriculum," "assessment," "instruction," and "professional development" across the top of the visual.
- In brief phrases, summarize the answers to the following questions: What was the curriculum five to eight years ago? (Put your response in the left-hand column) What is the current curriculum? (Put your response in the middle column on the same line.) If we implement curriculum mapping, what will the curriculum be? (Put your response in the right-hand column on the same line.)
- In a similar fashion, ask the team to answer the same questions as they relate to the other areas: assessment, instruction, and professional development. For each component, start a new line and respond to the same questions as you did with "curriculum This will help the team to see the evolution of each component.

Curriculum Mapping as a hub (group discussion)

- At your tables, discuss how curriculum mapping can serve as a hub for school improvement. You may find it helpful to go back to the visual you developed in "Connecting the Initiatives."
- Report your key points in the large group.

ASSIGNMENTS

- Think about changes that have occurred in your school system that have "lasted." What was there about the support structure or implementation process that made them "stick" while other initiatives have come and gone? Bring these thoughts to the next training session.
- Generate a list of current committees in your school. How might they support curriculum mapping in their work? Bring this information to the next training session.
- Conduct a Web search and preview different types of mapping software that are available. Begin to brainstorm a set of questions you would want addressed. Bring them to the next training session.

RESOURCES

Hale, J. (2007). *A Guide to Curriculum Mapping*. Thousand Oaks, CA: Corwin Press.

Hyerle, D. (2008). *Visual Tools for Transforming Information into Knowledge*. Thousand Oaks, CA: Corwin Press.

Jacobs, H.H. (1997). *Mapping the Big Picture: Integrating Curriculum and Assessment K–12*. Alexandria, VA: ASCD.

Jacobs, H.H. (2004). *Getting Results with Curriculum Mapping*. Alexandria, VA: ASCD. Chapters 1–2.

Jacobs, H.H. (2007). Resources on Web site—www.curriculumdesigners.com

Jacobs, H.H. (in press). *Curriculum 21: Essential Education for a Changing World*. Alexandria, VA: ASCD.

Kallick, B., and Colosimo, J. (2008) *Using Curriculum Mapping and Assessment Data to Improve Learning*. Thousand Oaks, CA: Corwin Press.

Udelhofen, S. (2005). *Keys to Curriculum Mapping: Strategies and Tools to Make It Work*. Thousand Oaks, CA: Corwin Press. Chapter 1.

Creating a Vision
for Your School or District

Educational visions need to be customized for the real students and their teachers in actual places. Generic vision statements cannot function! Prior to starting mapping in your school or district, clarify the desired end results to minimize confusion throughout the implementation process. What would curriculum mapping look like in your school or district when operationalized? What are your greatest hopes as a result of implementing mapping in your system? What would be different in one year? In two to three years? These are viable considerations as schools or districts continue their work together to "lay the foundation" for mapping by creating a common shared vision.

In addition to addressing identified needs, schools or districts discover that vision making is influenced by both internal and external factors (e.g., local, state, and federal mandates; board goals; time; resources) that establish parameters and impact the desired outcomes. All of these factors serve as filters or lenses in the development process.

So why take the time to create your vision? Defining your destination and determining the end results so that you can assess your progress along the way serves as a visual road map for all stakeholders. It becomes the story of your journey. The formation of this visual map represents the connection with other initiatives and aspects of the system and provides a powerful cornerstone for the mapping work. When developed collaboratively with stakeholders in the system it is a shared vision that provides both a short- and long-term focus for the school or district. Without a vision, mapping can become a lot of short day trips that lack the cohesive structure and substance of a well-orchestrated journey.

Purpose and Primary Focus

Module 3 focuses on the critical points a school or district needs to consider as it works collaboratively to develop a vision for mapping. Questions that will be addressed include: What are realistic goals? Where would you find the time to map? What will the elements in the maps be called in your school or district? What consistent terminology will be used in your school or district? What will the format look like? What types of maps will your school or district develop? What resources would be needed for successful implementation? How can mapping be used as a tool for improved student achievement? What are the potential benefits of mapping? How can feedback systems be structured to improve student achievement?

Activities and Supporting Materials

The activities in Module 3 are designed to engage participants in the process of developing a vision. As participants work to create their shared vision, they will explore how value-added changes, setting goals, time, differentiated professional development, the support structure, the feedback structure, the benefits of mapping, and technological support all influence it. They also will examine how the approach they take when they initiate the process of mapping affects the vision for mapping.

Many schools and districts already have packed calendars, so once they make a decision to move forward with mapping they need to think about what is doable in the allotted time. Trying to pack too much in too little time will only set mapping up for failure. If a school or district has already planned all upcoming inservice training, a realistic goal might be to implement a study group of key individuals who can develop some sample maps and also help leaders think through a roll-out plan for the next school year. It is also important to consider what you want to accomplish both short and long term.

What types of maps will your school create? Will you choose to start with individual maps or consensus maps? If you start with individual maps, will you use diary maps or projection maps? These decisions, too, must be made early in the process. Ideally, a school or district would start with individual maps and map what is currently being taught in every classroom, and then use the data from the review process to begin consensus maps for all grades and subjects. Sometimes internal and external factors dictate the starting point.

Setting realistic goals is critical to success. Unfortunately, sometimes local, state, or national mandates affect time lines. That is why even though there are better and more pure ways to start the mapping process, a school sometimes has to be creative in the approach. The key is to keep focused on the purpose of curriculum mapping and the intended outcomes so that ultimately you can reach the same rich results.

Four Schools. . . Four Approaches

Here are four possible approaches that leadership teams can consider as they identify the approach they will use in their own school or district. The examples we have included show how schools or districts have aligned the mapping process to address the needs in their system.

After making a collaborative decision with representatives from their staff to implement curriculum mapping, **the first school** trained teachers in the development of individual maps. The teachers mapped what they were actually teaching and then conducted a read through to identify gaps and repetitions. Once they had this data, the teachers were energized to make the needed changes to sharpen the alignment in their maps and to work collaboratively with other members of their grade, team, or subject to develop consensus maps for all grades and subjects.

The second school chose to implement curriculum mapping because it was notified by its state that its students had not reached their performance goals for that year. The district members encountered further complications because they hadn't actually reached the goals for the past three years. As much as they wanted to start with individual maps, they couldn't because they needed to ensure that a solid core curriculum was in place across the district. They began the process by developing consensus maps. Because the district didn't have an articulated curriculum, staff soon became energized as they saw a document evolve that would provide the focus they needed and wanted. Several staff members commented, "We finally know what we are supposed to be teaching." Once they had the consensus maps developed, they used them as a cornerstone for developing their individual maps.

A third school opted to start mapping through its curriculum review process because its inservice days were already planned for the year. Teachers on the review team in this school mapped the math curriculum and used it as tool to revise and update the curriculum. This provided a win-win solution. When they were ready to start mapping formally at the beginning of the next school year, there were 15 teachers who had had initial training in mapping through their work on the Curriculum Review Committee and were able to support other staff in the process.

A fourth school was in the process of revamping its assessment system. The teachers and administrators used mapping as a vehicle to refine their assessments. As they reviewed their assessment system, they "unpacked" the skills and content that students needed to know and demonstrate to be successful. This led to the development of maps and allowed them to sharpen their curricular focus in all areas and address gaps and repetitions in their system.

Sometimes you have to start where you can start! It may not be how you want to begin the process, but the strength of curriculum mapping is that because it is systemic in nature, it allows you to enter it at different points along the way. Be clear about the vision for mapping in your school or district. Your entry point into curriculum mapping is the basis for clearly defining your goals for mapping for both the short and long term.

Other Activities to Support the Development of the Vision

Rethinking your leadership support structure is another key to successful implementation. By thinking through the role of administrators, leadership teams, mentors, department chairs, and teacher leaders in the implementation of curriculum mapping, a school or district is laying a strong foundation for change. How does each leadership group support the process? What training do the leadership groups need to be successful in their roles? Are there other individuals who could be groomed as leaders to help sustain long-term change? These are important questions to consider as schools think about their leadership structure.

Technological support is also extremely important in the mapping process. Defining the vision for curriculum mapping will help schools or districts determine the guiding questions they need to consider when selecting the right technology. What will be different in your school or district a year from now? Two years from now? Five years from now? If a school or district hopes to use mapping as a process to align all aspects of the system, including the curriculum, assessments, instructional practices, and reporting tools, this will greatly impact the decision. Any technology decisions made by a school or district to support mapping efforts should support its long-term commitment and include the curriculum, assessments, instructional practices, and reporting tools.

Schools and districts need to be careful not to underestimate the importance of clearly defining the guiding questions up front to ensure they make the right decision. Both Heidi Hayes Jacobs and Bena Kallick have generated questions regarding technological support that you and your team might find helpful as you begin this conversation. Many schools and districts have made hasty decisions that cost them a lot in the end. Whether you choose not-for-profit or for profit or have a small group of stakeholders, carefully consider your options. The five leading mapping software vendors are all comprised of education and technology professionals of real integrity. All five require that teachers enter their own data by the actual school calendar and that those teachers and administrators can have access to each other's maps. The differences are the additional functions, which vary a great deal.

Different schools and districts have varying needs and it is best for you to consider this when making a decision. Arrange for demonstrations either on site or via WebEx (which, by the way, can be handled online and by phone). Things to consider include

1. The extent to which you need to see compiled data from many maps.
2. The nature of the reports and summaries you need.
3. Search possibilities—consider every angle for searching the maps that you think will be necessary for your faculty and administrators.
4. Alignment features with standards.
5. Lesson plan features.
6. Ease of use.
7. Possibilities for hyperlinks.
8. Technology support.
9. Training support.
10. Means of linking with student performance data.
11. Upcoming versions and new features.

When working with vendors, you need to be sure to work closely with their trainers to align the professional development work in mapping so there is consistency in expectations and terminology. This will help ensure a smooth transition.

Will the questions explored in this module change over the next few years as your school or district gains a deeper understanding of curriculum mapping? And more importantly, will your vision change? Most likely, yes, so it is important that your vision has room to evolve. That is why the feedback spiral is so critical to this process. Any quality system relies on data and research to keep it responsive to the needs of individuals in its organization.

Training Tips

Before making a decision regarding software, you may find it helpful to go online and collect information regarding different companies that provide curriculum mapping software. You may also find it helpful to contact other schools to find out what technology they are using to support mapping and the strengths and limitations they have discovered in the implementation process.

Online Materials

To use this module, you'll need to access the following online documents:

Module 3, Figure 1: Role of Administrators in the Mapping Process

Module 3, Figure 2: Roles and Responsibilities of Curriculum Teacher Leaders

Module 3, Figure 3: Benefits of Curriculum Maps

Module 3, Figure 4: Setting Goals

ESSENTIAL QUESTIONS

- How can mapping be used as a tool to develop a vision for improved student achievement?
- What are the potential benefits of curriculum mapping?
- How can feedback systems be structured to improve student achievement?

CONTENT

Concept: The mapping process can be used by a school or district to create a vision for the future and serve as a connector to focus all aspects of the system on school improvement.

- Value-Added Changes
- Setting Goals
- Time
- Differentiated Professional Development
- The Support Structure
- Feedback Structure
- Benefits of Mapping
- Technological Support—A Comparative Examination
- **TERMS** Differentiated Professional Development, Support Structures

SKILLS

- Identify possible value-added changes that could occur in your school or district if curriculum mapping were implemented.
- Develop possible short- and long-term goals.
- Identify time that can be used for training.
- Brainstorm the different types of professional development needed to ensure successful implementation.
- Identify potential school or district leaders who could help implement the mapping process.
- Clarify roles and responsibilities for leadership groups.
- Identify training the leaders would need to provide support for mapping.
- Develop an evaluation structure to provide ongoing feedback to modify and strengthen the implementation process.
- Identify potential benefits for different stakeholders in the school or district.
- Develop essential questions to guide the selection of curriculum mapping software.

EVIDENCE OF LEARNING

- List of value-added changes
- Short- and long-term goals
- Brainstorm list of possible ways to find time
- List of training needed to ensure successful implementation
- A grid that shows a possible leadership structure including: groups or individuals, roles and responsibilities, and training needs
- Types of feedback and possible tools, processes, or structures that could be used to collect it
- Graphic organizer that identifies potential benefits for each stakeholder group
- Essential questions to guide technology selection

ACTIVITIES

Value-Added Changes (small group discussion)
- In small groups, identify what might be different in one to three years if you were to implement curriculum mapping. What would it look like? What would be in place? What would be different in classrooms?
- Share your thoughts in the large group.
- Identify tentative goals for year 1, year 2, and long term. List the goals on a sheet of paper.
- After each goal, identify what you would accept as evidence that the goal has been successfully achieved.

Dealing with Time (large group and individual and/or team activity)
- Begin as a large group, and brainstorm chunks of time that could be used for training in your school or district. Think creatively.
- In your teams, discuss alternatives that might work best for your school or district.
- Identify specific chunks of time that could be used in your school or district.
- Go back and revisit your goal for year 1. Based on the amount of time you have available to focus on mapping, is your goal realistic?
- Make any needed adjustments based on the actual amount of time you will have to devote to mapping.

Professional Development (team and group exercise)
- In your school or district teams, brainstorm the different types of training that members of your staff would need to be successful in implementing curriculum mapping.
- Capture your thoughts on chart paper.
- Post your charts and conduct a gallery walk.
- Discuss types of professional development that were identified on the sheets and how schools and districts might be able to differentiate the training to accommodate the needs of all learners.

Rethinking Your Leadership Structure (individual or team exercise)
- Make 4 columns on a piece of chart paper.
- Brainstorm possible committees, leaders, or leadership groups that could help provide support in the implementation process. List them in column 1 on a sheet of chart paper.
- After each group, list their current responsibilities in column 2.
- In the third column, identify the roles they could play in the implementation process.
- In the fourth column, identify training they would need to ensure success with their new responsibilities.

The Feedback Spiral (small and large discussion)
- Beginning in small groups, brainstorm types of feedback that would be helpful as a school or district works to implement the process of curriculum mapping. Consider the different phases of implementation. Where would feedback be particularly helpful in fine-tuning the process? What kind of feedback would be most helpful at that stage of the process?

- Brainstorm different tools, processes, or structures that could be used to get that feedback.
- Share in the larger group.

Benefits (small group exercise)
- Using the "Benefits of Curriculum Maps" organizer provided in the training module, have table groups each focus on a different stakeholders' group (i.e., students, parents, community members, and teachers) and ask them to brainstorm a list of possible benefits for their assigned group.
- Record them on the organizer.
- Share specific benefits from each group.
- Discuss the common themes that surface.
- As a large group, discuss any other benefits you would add to any of the categories.

Selecting Technology (small group jigsaw and processing)
- In small groups, jigsaw pages 69–74 in *Keys to Curriculum Mapping*.
- After reading and sharing the information provided, brainstorm as a group what your school or district would need from a technology system that would support curriculum mapping.
- Use the identified short- and long-term goals for curriculum mapping as a filter to help refine your expectations.
- Brainstorm a list of questions that could be used with vendors to see if they can meet your needs both short term and long term.

ASSIGNMENTS

- Using the sample maps in Module 4 as an example, begin to map the content and skills for an upcoming unit, and bring it to the next training session.
- Identify the main concept that serves as the connector for your unit, and bring it to the next training session.

RESOURCES

Costa, A., and Kallick, B. (1995). *Assessment in the Learning Organization.* Alexandria, VA: ASCD. Pages 25–31.

Hale, J. (2007). *A Guide to Curriculum Mapping.* Thousand Oaks, CA: Corwin Press. Chapters 10 and 12.

Jacobs, H.H. (1997). *Mapping the Big Picture: Integrating Curriculum and Assessment K–12.* Alexandria, VA: ASCD.

Jacobs, H.H. (2004). *Getting Results with Curriculum Mapping.* Alexandria, VA: ASCD. Chapters 4 and 6.

Jacobs, H.H. (2007). Resources on Web site—www.curriculumdesigners.com

Jacobs, H.H. (in press). *Curriculum 21: Essential Education for a Changing World.* Alexandria, VA: ASCD.

Udelhofen, S. (2005). *Keys to Curriculum Mapping: Strategies and Tools to Make It Work.* Thousand Oaks, CA: Corwin Press. Chapter 5.

Wiggins, G., and McTighe, J. (2007). *Schooling by Design.* Alexandria, VA: ASCD. Chapters 2, 3, 7, 8, and 9.

II.

Launching the
PROCESS

Ensuring Long-Term Support: Revising School Based Decision-Making Structures

How are curriculum decisions made in your school or district? Who are the key players in the decision-making process? How do those decisions reach the students? As schools or districts begin to address the curricular needs in their system, staff members often are confused regarding where and how the decisions are made. In fact, staff members, when asked, frequently say they really don't know how these decisions are made. Vagueness can lead to finger pointing, an unwillingness to accept responsibility, and increased uncertainty which simply translates into a nebulous vision that becomes an obstacle to substantive change. If support structures like decision making and leadership are not clearly defined and understood by staff, they become major stumbling blocks in the implementation process. The lack of clarity can compound confusion and hamper the positive interaction and communication that is needed for this process to have its greatest effect on student achievement. The practical and inspirational work by the DuFours on Professional Learning Communities can provide a context for strong and efficient communication.

Schools or districts can use the process of curriculum mapping to examine the effectiveness of their existing decision-making process and the leadership support structure. Curriculum mapping also can be used to examine the key programmatic structures that also influence curriculum and instruction decision making such as schedule (daily, annual, and long term), grouping of students (within classrooms, throughout the institution, and by class size), grouping of personnel (into teams, departments, and roles), and space (both physical location and virtual space). As schools or districts begin to map and analyze their support structures, they often find gaps and overlaps in the structures that hamper communication and limit their effectiveness. In many systems, the structures are well-kept secrets. No one seems to know quite how they function or if they do function. Tightening the alignment in these structures and clarifying roles and responsibilities will strengthen communication throughout the system. The system is then able to better maximize the use of these structures to provide the needed support vital to ensuring a guaranteed, relevant, and rigorous curriculum for all students in the system. You will be able to eliminate unnecessary groups and meetings and you can begin to virtually carry out the curriculum planning via software.

If aligned and clearly articulated, decision-making structures and processes become more transparent. When this happens they provide the solid framework needed to sustain change and provide the support to staff to keep a school or district on course during the implementation process.

Purpose and Primary Focus

The content in Module 4 is intended to provide strategies to help leaders and leadership teams analyze the effectiveness of their school or district's current decision-making structures so they can make the most of the structures when implementing systemic change. Are the right groups involved in the decision-making process? What are their roles and responsibilities? What is the role of current committees in your school or district? How could the current committees in your school or district assume some of these roles and responsibilities? How do current structures (e.g., schedules, or groupings) impact the decision-making process? Are there ways the current structure could be realigned to streamline efforts and provide greater support? These are some of the questions that will be explored in more depth.

Activities and Supporting Materials

Activities are focused on important points that need to be considered when analyzing and rethinking support structures. Areas of focus include:

- Organizational Structures for School Based Decision Making (i.e., PLCs, cabinets, councils)
- Grouping of Personnel (i.e., vertical planning teams, cross-disciplinary teams, horizontal teams, departments)

- Targeted Work Groups
- Grouping of Students (i.e. within classrooms, throughout the institutions, and by class size)
- Design Strategies for Schedules (i.e., daily, annual, long term)
- Time Lines for Developing Site-Based Teaching and Learning Structures

During the workshop, participants have an opportunity to work through a gap analysis process to review the current status, determine the desired status, and identify the changes that need to be made to maximize their benefits.

Training Tips

Mapping as a hub for school improvement provides the cornerstone for meaningful professional development leading to differentiated opportunities for staff. It is much like going to the eye doctor. When you are seated in the chair and he or she is trying lens after lens to help sharpen your vision. "This one…or this one. Number one or number two…." When you find the right lens (structure), it can crystallize and strengthen your performance in all areas.

In addition to the activities provided in this module, participants are encouraged to read *Getting Results with Curriculum Mapping*. In the last chapter, Heidi suggests additional activities that can provide support to schools or districts that are working to revise their school-based decision-making structures.

Online Materials

To use this module, you'll need to access the following online document:

Module 4, Figure 1: System Influences on Curriculum Teaching

ESSENTIAL QUESTIONS
- What school based structures will ensure long-term support in your school or district?
- If not committees, then what?
- How do structures impact the curriculum?

CONTENT

Concept: An efficient decision-making structure can help to ensure successful long-term implementation.

- Organizational Structures for School Based Decision Making (e.g., cabinets, councils, or PLCs)
- Grouping of Personnel (e.g., vertical planning teams, cross-disciplinary teams, horizontal teams, departments.)
- Targeted Work Groups
- Grouping of Students (e.g., within classrooms, throughout the institutions, and by class size)
- Design Strategies for Schedules (e.g., daily, annual, or long term)
- Time Lines for Developing Site Based Teaching and Learning Structures
- **TERMS** Professional Learning Committees (PLCs), School Based Support Structures, Targeted Work Groups

SKILLS
- Identify sample organizational structures for school based decision making.
- Compare and contrast different types of organizational structures.
- Determine roles and responsibilities.
- Create a grouping structure for your school personnel that would support mapping in your school or district.
- Brainstorm possible uses of targeted work groups.
- Identify ways that the grouping of students impacts curriculum, instruction, and assessment.
- Summarize the impact of different schedules on curriculum, instruction, and assessment.
- Develop an organizational structure and time line for your school or district that will support mapping.

EVIDENCE OF LEARNING
- A diagram of the current school or district structures, roles, and responsibilities
- Suggested grouping structures for personnel
- List of possible targeted work groups to support mapping
- Key points from the discussion on grouping of students and the impact on curriculum
- Key points from discussion on schedules and the impact on curriculum, instruction, and assessment
- Grouping structure for your school or district
- Proposed structure for school based decision making, time line, and roles

Organizational Structure for School Based Decision Making (workshop and small group processing)

- Read Chapters 6 and 7 in *Mapping the Big Picture* and Chapter 10 in *Getting Results with Curriculum Mapping* on organizational structures for school based decision making.
- In small groups, discuss the key points.
- Then, share with a partner the draft structure that you developed in the activity "Rethinking Your Leadership Structure" (in Module 3). Are there any changes you might make to strengthen the structure?

Grouping of Personnel (jigsaw activity)

- In small groups, jigsaw pages 126–132 from *Getting Results with Curriculum Mapping*.
- Work as a table team or divide into school or district teams and create a grouping structure for personnel that you feel would support mapping in a school or district.
- Share with other colleagues.

Targeted Work Groups (discussion and brainstorming activity)

- Discuss the purpose of targeted work groups.
- At your table, brainstorm possible targeted work groups that could be used in the mapping process to help support implementation.
- Share in the large group.

Groupings of Students (discussion in small grade level groups)

- Divide into grade-level groups—elementary (K–2), upper elementary, middle school or junior high, and high school.
- In your level groups, brainstorm the different groupings of students that are used in your schools or districts.
- List them on chart paper. Discuss the potential impact on curriculum, instruction, and assessment.
- Share in the large group.

Schedules, Schedules, Who's Got the Schedule (small group discussion)

- Brainstorm the different types of schedules that exist in the schools and districts at your table. Discuss the impact they have on curriculum, assessment, and instruction.

Rethinking our Structure (team exercise)

- In your school or district team, develop a draft organizational structure for school based decision making for your school or district. Identify the roles and responsibilities for each group.
- Also, identify the time line needed to implement the structure.
- Share your draft with another team.

ASSIGNMENTS

- Read Chapter 2 in *Getting Results with Curriculum Mapping* (see resources) in preparation for the next training session.
- Think about . . . What are the nonnegotiables in your curriculum?
- Go to the Web and pull a copy of the national standards for your area and a set of standards and benchmarks from your state, a neighboring state, or a school. Bring these copies to the next session.

RESOURCES

Hale, J. (2007). *A Guide to Curriculum Mapping*. Thousand Oaks, CA: Corwin Press. Chapter 1.

Jacobs, H.H. (1997). *Mapping the Big Picture: Integrating Curriculum and Assessment K–12*. Alexandria, VA: ASCD.

Jacobs, H.H. (2004). *Getting Results with Curriculum Mapping*. Alexandria, VA: ASCD. Chapter 10.

Jacobs, H.H. (2007). *Active Literacy Across the Curriculum*. Larchmont, NY: Eye on Education.

Jacobs, H.H. (2007). Resources on Web site—www.curriculumdesigners.com

Jacobs, H.H. (in press). *Curriculum 21: Essential Education for a Changing World*. Alexandria, VA: ASCD.

Kallick, B., and Colosimo, J. (2007). *Using Curriculum Mapping and Assessment Data to Improve Learning*. Thousand Oaks, CA: Corwin Press.

Udelhofen, S. (2005). *Keys to Curriculum Mapping: Strategies and Tools to Make It Work*. Thousand Oaks, CA: Corwin Press. Chapter 2.

Wiggins, G., and McTighe, J. (2007). *Schooling by Design*. Alexandria, VA: ASCD.

Creating Individual Maps

Designing quality maps sets the stage for success. If the data entered in the maps are of high quality, they provide the foundation for powerful, rich professional discussions about teaching and learning and launch the process of curriculum mapping.

In our first module, we established the importance of recognizing each of the basic elements in a map. Individual maps contain essential questions, content, skills, and assessments. Essential questions provide focus for the unit, push students to higher levels of thinking, and help to make connections across curricular areas. Grant Wiggins and Jay McTighe, authors of *Understanding by Design* (2005) and noted leaders in the field of curriculum reform, ask us to consider, "What types of questions might guide our teaching and engage students in uncovering the important ideas at the heart of each subject?" when designing essential questions. Content refers to the "what" that is to be taught. It includes a main concept or idea that provides focus for instruction. Concepts are relational statements such as: a country's geography determines the economic possibilities. As teachers clearly articulate the concept, they are able to "unpack" the specific content that needs to be taught for students to demonstrate understanding of the concept. The content section also includes key vocabulary that is required to have successful understanding of the content. Skills, which are directly aligned with the essential questions and the content, begin with action verbs and identify the precise proficiencies students need to know and be able to demonstrate. The assessments are the demonstrations of learning performances or exhibitions. They allow the students to show you what they know.

As schools become more involved in the mapping process, many have expanded their maps to include other elements, such as activities resources and materials, and instructional strategies.

Creating quality individual maps takes time. By understanding the components, teachers need to be taught strategies to sharpen the alignment between the elements in an individual map. Teaching how to map is far more than showing a set of overview slides and then telling the staff to develop their maps for a year. It involves breaking the process down into manageable pieces, modeling the "how tos," sharing exemplars so teachers have a clear picture of quality, and providing meaningful feedback. The most important word in staff development is "feedback." To help you give quality feedback, we have included coaching protocols. We recommend that all members of the mapping community study these protocols during the process.

Clarity in the task is critical for success. I'm reminded of a college course I took in which a professor assigned a major project. Because the task was poorly explained and there wasn't a clear sense of what "it" was, students were constantly taking drafts up to him and asking, "Is this what you want?" "Is this what you mean?" "Am I on the right track?" To ensure high-quality work, take the time to make sure the teachers know what "it" is.

Purpose and Primary Focus

Module 5 provides the basic tools and strategies to help teams develop high-quality maps. Guiding questions used to focus this module include: What constitutes a quality map? Why does it matter? and Who should map?

Activities and Supporting Materials

The activities and supporting materials included in Module 5 build on the activities from Module 1, when participants had an opportunity to look at different types of sample maps. By examining a number of maps in various stages of development in that activity, participants were able to begin to think about a number of questions: What makes one map better than another? Which maps provided more useful data? Which elements in the maps were more precise? The activities in Module 5 use the information gleaned from the slides and the sample map activity in Module 1 as a basis for design work. You will find the coaching protocols helpful in guiding your review.

One strategy that is included in this module is called "Unpacking the Standards." Bena Kallick, Karen Bailey, and other consultants have used this strategy in many of their workshops. It entails taking a standard and unpacking it to clearly define the specific content and skills that are embedded in the standard. By using this process, maps demonstrate greater clarity because of the precision in language in the content, skills, assessments, and essential questions. The "Unpacking the Standards" strategy coupled with a "step-by-step" approach to thinking through the development of individual maps encourages participants to use precise language as they practice alignment strategies. A facilitator may use the step-by-step approach to coach teachers in small groups or individually to develop their own quality one-month maps.

They then have an opportunity to form pairs or triads to practice their coaching skills using the curriculum mapping protocols. As they review each other's maps, they can focus on key questions such as: Is there enough information on the map to have a clear understanding of what is being taught at that grade level or subject? Is the language clear? Are the components aligned?

At some point as leaders begin to think about implementing curriculum mapping in their school or district, they will wrestle with the question of who should map. It may appear like a simple question, but what if you are an elementary teacher who supports a dozen students in different grades with reading or math difficulties. Do you develop curriculum maps? What if you are a teacher in an English as a Second Language class that uses a canned curriculum? Do you develop a curriculum map? And what about the high school counselor whose primary focus is to serve as an advisor? What should they map? In addition to the activities included in this module, additional samples can be found at www.curriculumdesigners.com.

It all goes back to one question: What's the purpose of curriculum mapping?

Training Tips

As mentioned previously, external factors can influence your starting point in the mapping process. Depending on whether you begin with individual maps or consensus maps will determine whether you begin with Module 5 or Module 7 (Developing Consensus Maps).

For that reason, you may find it helpful to read through the information in both modules before beginning this work.

In Module 7, we talk about the use of quality filters to help ensure the development of exemplary consensus maps. Quality filters are simply samples or exemplars from other schools and national organizations. In addition to using the suggested mapping protocols, you may also find the use of the filters or lenses suggested in Module 7 helpful in coaching for high-quality maps. These samples can be helpful when you need help with wording, the infusion of higher order thinking, and the infusion of 21st century skills. They are helpful in providing ideas and starting points. Care should be taken when using them not to assume that they are all-inclusive or the final answer to mapping. The best maps are the maps that are developed internally through rich, professional discussions that reflect the values, beliefs, and needs of students in your school or district.

Coaching tools that can be very helpful to teachers as they work to integrate higher order thinking in the maps can be found in Web sites that feature the work of leaders in the field like Benjamin Bloom and Art Costa.

Another source that can be extremely valuable is Heidi's book, *Active Literacy Across the Curriculum*. High-quality maps, both individual and consensus, not only include the curricular skills but also include the critical cross-curricular skills such as literacy skills, higher order thinking skills, problem solving skills, and research and information processing skills, along with other skills students will need in the 21st century. These filters are elaborated on in Modules 9 and 12.

A final thought to consider before beginning these activities is *do not underestimate the power of modeling*. Some of the most effective workshops are simply breaking the task down and working through the development of a map together using chart paper and markers. When you have a chance to talk through the process and teachers hear your thinking as you work through the process together, it can help clarify questions and issues that may be preventing high-quality maps.

Online Materials

To use this module, you'll need to access the following online documents:

Module 5, Figure 1: Unpacking Standards

Module 5, Figure 2: Coaching Protocols

ESSENTIAL QUESTIONS

- What constitutes a quality map?
- Why does it matter?
- Who should map?

CONTENT

Concept: Coaching strategies can ensure high-quality curriculum maps.

- Unpacking Standards
- The Concept and Content
- Alignment of Skills
- Bi-Level Thinking: Integration of 21st Century Skills
- Aligning Assessments
- Essential Questions
- Coaching Protocols to Ensure Quality
- Calibrating the Process for Teachers Who Teach Special Populations
- **TERMS** Alignment, Assessments, Benchmark Skills, Bi-Level Thinking, Coaching Protocols, Concept, Content, Diary Maps, Essential Questions, Individual Maps, Non-Negotiables, Power Standards, Projection Maps, Unpacking Standards, Standards, Skills, 21st Century Skills

SKILLS

- Unpack standards to identify precision content and skills.
- Develop quality maps using a step-by-step process.
- Identify a concept to focus content.
- Use development tools (e.g., verb sheets, developmentally appropriate activities, etc.) to ensure the inclusion of higher level performance).
- Integrate 21st century skills.
- Unpack assessments to test alignment with content, skills, and essential questions.
- Use coaching strategies to develop quality essential questions.
- Use coaching protocols to ensure high-quality maps.
- Tailor process to address the needs of special populations.

EVIDENCE OF LEARNING

- Sample standards your team has unpacked
- One-month maps with essential questions, concept/content, skills, and assessments
- Sample concepts and content
- Maps that have integrated bi-level skills
- Feedback and highlights from the coaching sessions
- Modifications for special populations

ACTIVITIES

"Unpacking Standards" (small group exercise)

- In like curricular groups, identify a standard for your area.
- As a team, brainstorm the specific content embedded in that standard.
- Next, identify the precise skills needed to demonstrate understanding of that standard.
- Continue this process with other standards in your area. You may find the "Unpacking the Big Ideas" template (Module 5, Figure 1) helpful in organizing your thoughts as you unpack a specific standard.

Creating Quality Maps (workshop)

- After reading Chapter 3 in *Keys to Curriculum Mapping* or chapters 4 and 5 in *A Guide to Curriculum Mapping*, identify the elements in a map.
- What are the key points to keep in mind when developing a map?
- What questions do you have?

Developing Individual Maps (work session)

- Divide into like curricular areas. In small groups, work together to develop one-month maps. You can revise a map you developed for the assignment to prepare for the training session or you can start a new unit.
- Begin by focusing on a major concept that is at the heart of your unit. Write it in the content section of the map.
- After identifying the concept, identify the content you will need to teach so that the students can demonstrate their understanding of the concept. List the content under the concept.
- Next, identify the skills that students need to be able to demonstrate in relationship to the content. Consider the level of understanding the students need to perform. Use the verb sheets provided in the training module to check for the desired level of understanding. Also, consider integrated skills that could be incorporated to reinforce critical cross-curricular skills such as literacy and technology.
- Identify assessments that align with the skills and allow the students to demonstrate their understanding of the content and skills. Consider including a variety of assessment types to include a more complete picture of learning.
- Once you have identified the assessments, unpack them to cross-check skills needed to be successful. Are they included in the skills section?

Participants may find the coaching protocols (Module 5, Figure 3) helpful as they work to develop their maps.

Essential Questions (workshop and small group exercise)

- Using the information from Chapters 4 and 5 in *Keys to Curriculum Mapping*, the coaching protocols provided in the materials, and Chapter 5 in *Understanding by Design*, discuss the criteria for quality essential questions.
- In your groups, work to develop quality essential questions for your unit(s).

Critical Friends (small group coaching exercise)

- Work in teams of two or three people. Take turns sharing your map, while the other person(s) use(s) the coaching protocols to help you think about quality elements.
- Your role as a coach is to ask open-ended questions that will help your colleagues think about their map from another perspective so they can make the language in the map as precise as possible.
- As a team, you are working together to make them precise and of high quality.

Addressing Challenges in Special Populations (small and large group discussion)

- In the large group, list curricular areas that may need to be adjusted or modified.
- In small groups, take an assigned area and generate a possible solution that will maintain the integrity of the mapping process and meet the unique needs of special populations with whom they may work.
- Share your area(s) in the large group.

ASSIGNMENTS

- Use the strategies you have learned in this module to refine and continue the development of your year-long map. If you are a staff developer or administrator, map an in-service or a faculty meeting.
- As you work on your draft map, think about how or when you might be able to reinforce literacy skills such as reading strategies, vocabulary, speaking, etc.
- Prior to the next session, make copies of your map for your read through team. Use the focus areas in the quadrants on the feedback form for the read through process (in the supporting documents for Module 6) as a guide for reading your team members' maps prior to the session. Feel free to jot notes on their maps as you look for possible gaps, repetitions, etc. Bring these to the next training session.

RESOURCES

Erickson, L. (2002). *Concept-based Curriculum and Instruction: Teaching Beyond the Facts.* Thousand Oaks, CA: Corwin Press.

Hale, J. (2007). *A Guide to Curriculum Mapping.* Thousand Oaks, CA: Corwin Press. Chapters 4–5.

Jacobs, H.H. (1997). *Mapping the Big Picture: Integrating Curriculum and Assessment K–12.* Alexandria, VA: ASCD.

Jacobs, H.H. (2004). *Getting Results with Curriculum Mapping.* Alexandria, VA: ASCD. Chapters 2 and 9.

Jacobs, H.H. (2007). *Active Literacy Across the Curriculum: Strategies for Reading, Writing, Speaking, and Listening.* Larchmont, NY: Eye on Education. Chapters 1–9.

Jacobs, H.H. (2007). Resources on Web site—www.curriculumdesigners.com

Jacobs, H.H. (in press). *Curriculum 21: Essential Education for a Changing World.* Alexandria, VA: ASCD. Chapters 2, 4, and 5.

McTighe, J., and Wiggins, G. (2005). *Understanding by Design.* Alexandria, VA: ASCD. Chapters 1–7.

Udelhofen, S. (2005). *Keys to Curriculum Mapping: Strategies and Tools to Make It Work.* Thousand Oaks, CA: Corwin Press. Chapters 2, 3, and 4.

Initiating the Review Cycle:
The Read Through Process

Mapping is a verb. It is an active review process articulated in the Curriculum Mapping Seven-Step Review Process developed by Jacobs (1997). After developing maps, schools and districts enter the editing phase of the process, known as the read through. During this editing phase, schools or districts find teachers experience the purpose of curriculum mapping. Teachers who may not have been on board in the early stages frequently find themselves very engaged in the rich dialogues that come about as a result of the mapping process. They begin to understand how the maps can become the focal point around which meaningful professional discussions can take place in an efficient manner.

During this phase in the process, teachers have an opportunity to gain a deeper understanding of the curriculum by examining their colleagues' maps. They gain a better understanding of the curriculum across the system in addition to having the opportunity to "zoom in" on specific targeted areas. Teachers practice their editing skills as they review the maps for possible gaps, repetitions, and omissions. In addition, they also note questions they may have and clarifications needed to understand the content being taught in different classes or courses.

While this is an exciting, engaging process, it is not uncommon for teachers to feel somewhat vulnerable during this because since they are baring their souls by sharing what they believe to be most important in learning—their curriculum. For this reason, we have suggested some strategies that can be used to ensure a safe, respectful sharing environment that encourages these rich professional dialogues.

It is during this phase that teachers have the opportunity to truly experience the heart of the mapping process. It takes mapping to another level as teachers gain a clearer sense of the purpose of mapping and how it can be used as a tool to impact classroom instruction and student achievement. In short, *having* maps does not help learners—*using* them will.

Purpose and Primary Focus

Module 6 explains the Seven-Step Review Process and how it serves as a medium for rich professional discussions that can provide the data needed to strengthen alignment and provide a stronger curriculum for the children in their school or district. This module also includes strategies and suggestions to help set up a read through cycle and maximize the benefits from this phase in the mapping process. Key questions that are explored in this module include: How can the mapping process be used to revise the current curriculum in your school or district? What strategies can be used to maximize the benefits of the review cycle? What are the short- and long-term benefits of the review cycle?

Activities and Supporting Materials

Activities and supporting materials provided in this module focus on the Curriculum Mapping Seven-Step Review Process (Jacobs, 1997); the purpose of the cycle; types of read throughs; map reading strategies; review process protocols; data collection; prioritization of data findings; strategies to address the targets to be addressed; and benefits of the cycle.

Ideally, you begin with a mixed-group review that allows staff to get a big picture perspective by gaining a better understanding of the curriculum across the school. High school and middle school teams comprised of 6–10 teachers who represent different grades and curricular areas can gain invaluable insight into the broader curriculum through cross-group reviews. Elementary teachers who represent different grades and subjects can have rich discussions and see possible connections in other curricular areas. Teachers in the arts and in areas like special education add a unique perspective to the process and sometimes are able to see things that other teachers do not because they work across subjects and grade levels.

In our experience and research, we have found that the mixed-group review helps to provide a broad view of the curriculum. The broad-base perspective gained through a mixed-group review gives teachers new eyes through which to review the curriculum in their area.

It is important that staff be encouraged to look beyond their current curriculum and think about what would be more meaningful to the students and their future success. A mixed-group review encourages thinking towards "what should be," not "what is" or "what was." It is an opportunity to go beyond playing Trivial Pursuit in classrooms and focus on the big ideas and enduring understandings that are critical for students to know. Sometimes teachers have difficulty "letting go" of their curriculum long enough to see how it fits into the bigger picture if you start with a like-group review. For these reasons, if at all possible, start with mixed-group reviews.

Both kinds of reviews provide rich data and can help educators identify the strengths, gaps, repetitions, and areas where the articulation of skills may not be as strong. When groups have a chance to analyze the data during the revision process, they can identify revisions that need to be made in the curriculum. This in turn can lead to an organized plan to address the priority areas that surfaced during the read-through process, if they have opted to go with short sessions that focus on one area. For example, in one elementary school, they found that they were teaching note taking in most of the grades but using different formats. The principal allowed them to use a faculty meeting (one hour) after school. They sent out a note letting everyone know to bring their maps and that they were going to work on sequencing the teaching of note taking. By keeping the session focused, they were able to resolve this priority area in one hour and set the stage for further productive meetings.

Another school decided to focus on one of the priority areas in an after-school meeting. The teacher leaders in that building sent out a note to all teachers inviting them to attend. Unfortunately, they couldn't require it contractually. They were surprised when everyone but one person showed up with their maps in hand. Within the 45 minutes allotted, they resolved the issue. Teachers were so pleased to see progress being made, they decided to continue the 45-minute sessions.

Training Tips

The process is energizing because it provides the structure to make needed changes to provide a stronger curriculum for the students. A question that is often raised during training sessions is: Do maps have to be completed for a full year before we engage in the read-through process? The answer is no. Some schools have found the data they received from skills and content for a few months were invaluable in modifying the maps. This knowledge can also help to raise the level of quality in teachers' maps as they continue to work on them. Again, because you actually use the maps to gain information, this review process often provides a shot of energy that enables you to expand the process to include essential questions and assessments. At the end of the year, the schools conduct another review with the finished maps that gives them even more data around which to make instructional decisions.

Activities and materials included in Module 6 underscore the importance of the read-through cycle by showing you how to review maps through a common lens (i.e., the areas generated by the leadership team), how to set up the data collection phase of the cycle, and how to develop action plans to use the data to make instructional decisions.

Online Materials

To use this module, you'll need to access the following online documents:

Module 6, Figure 1: The CM Seven-Step Review Process

Module 6, Figure 2: Mixed-Group and Like-Group Review Protocol

Module 6, Figure 3: Coaching Questions and Stems

Module 6, Figure 4: Read Through Feedback Form 1

Module 6, Figure 5: Read Through Feedback Form 2

ESSENTIAL QUESTIONS

- How can the mapping process be used to revise the current curriculum in your school or district?
- What are the short- and long-term benefits of the review cycle?

CONTENT

Concept: The read through process provides the vehicle through which a school or district can make meaningful instructional decisions.

- The Seven-Step Review Process
- Purpose of the Review Cycle
- Reading Maps for Information
- Types of Read Throughs
- Protocols for Review Process
- Collection and Analysis of Data
- Determination of Priorities
- Strategies to Address Target Areas
- Benefits of the Review Cycle
- **TERMS** Like Coaching Group Review, Mixed Coaching Group Review, Coaching Protocols, Read Through Process, Review Cycle

SKILLS

- Summarize the Seven-Step Review Cycle.
- Distinguish between different types of read throughs.
- Use a protocol to implement the review cycle.
- Read maps for specific data/areas of focus.
- Collect and analyze data to determine immediate priorities.
- Generate strategies to address priorities.
- Develop a time line and determine next steps.
- Identify the benefits of the read through process.

EVIDENCE OF LEARNING

- Summary notes including: key points, purposes, and questions from the discussion on the Seven-Step Review Cycle
- Data collection charts from the different groups
- Analysis of data from the read through process with noted priorities
- Action plan to address the priorities identified
- List of benefits of the process

Seven-Step Review Cycle (workshop)

- Read Chapter 2 in Mapping the Big Picture and Chapters 7 and 8 in *A Guide to Curriculum Mapping,* which provide information on the Seven-Step Review Cycle.
- In table groups, synthesize the information shared and develop a visual (on chart paper) that summarizes the information. Be sure to include: the model, purpose, and types of read throughs.
- Discuss the merits of each of the different types of read throughs.
- Share your visual in the large group.

Read Through Process (small group exercise)

- In small groups, using the maps you generated during the last session and any additional months you have had an opportunity to complete, conduct the read through process using the protocol provided in the training module. (For this activity, sample maps could also be used to practice the process.)
- Follow the directions in the protocol and generate feedback on large poster sheets.
- When all groups have completed the process of generating the feedback for the targeted areas, post the sheets on the wall and conduct a gallery walk.

Analysis of Review Cycle Data (small group exercise)

- Following the gallery walk, in your read through groups, identify common themes that emerged.
- As a group, determine top priority areas.
- Share your common themes and priorities with the other groups. Is there consensus? If not, what can you do to reach consensus?

Action Plan/Time Line (small group exercise)

- In small groups, brainstorm possible ways to address the priority areas. Consider creative ways to find time, who should be involved, time lines, etc.
- Share suggestions in the larger group.

Processing the Benefits (small group exercise)

- In small groups, discuss benefits of the read through process. What worked? What changes would you make in the protocol for the next read through?
- Are there any other changes you would recommend for the next review?

ASSIGNMENTS

- Bring the list of your school or district committees that you developed for the third training module.
- Develop a draft of what you believe is the current organizational structure for school based decision making in your school or district. Bring it to the next training session.

RESOURCES

Costa, A., and Garmston, R. (2001). *Cognitive Coaching: A Foundation for Renaissance Schools.* Norwood, MA: Christopher Gordon.

Costa, A., and Garmston, R. (2008). Cognitive Coaching: Conversations That Mediate Self-Directedness. In A. Costa (Ed.), *The School as a Home for the Mind.* Thousand Oaks, CA: Corwin Press.

Hale, J. (2007). *A Guide to Curriculum Mapping.* Thousand Oaks, CA: Corwin Press. Chapters 7 and 8.

Jacobs, H.H. (1997). *Mapping the Big Picture: Integrating Curriculum and Assessment K–12.* Alexandria, VA: ASCD. Chapters 2–3.

Jacobs, H.H. (2004). *Getting Results with Curriculum Mapping.* Alexandria, VA: ASCD. Chapters 6 and 9.

Jacobs, H.H. (2007). Resources on Web site—www.curriculumdesigners.com

Jacobs, H.H. (2007). *Active Literacy Across the Curriculum.* Larchmont, NY: Eye on Education.

Jacobs, H.H. (in press). *Curriculum 21: Essential Education for a Changing World.* Alexandria, VA: ASCD. Chapters 2, 4, and 5.

Udelhofen, S. (2005). *Keys to Curriculum Mapping: Strategies and Tools to Make It Work.* Thousand Oaks, CA: Corwin Press. Pages 39–46.

Developing Consensus Maps

The Latin root word for consensus is *con cen tre* which means the acknowledgement of common truths. A consensus map reflects the policy agreed on by a professional staff and targets those specific areas in each discipline and across disciplines that are to be addressed with consistency and flexibility in a school or a district. The result of this professional decision is a consensus map. Consensus maps are sometimes also referred to as essential maps, core maps, district maps, or master maps. But, in essence, they are all the same in that they represent a collaborative decision regarding the consistent and flexible curriculum in a school or district.

The key for your school or district is to use consistent terminology to avoid needless confusion. Some schools or districts identify the information contained on the consensus maps as the nonnegotiables that will be taught in each grade or subject in a school or district. These nonnegotiables are determined by staff through a collaborative professional review and discussion. High-quality consensus maps integrate best practices, 21st century curriculum, higher order thinking, high standards, and clearly defined grade- or course-level expectations. At a minimum, the consensus maps include content and skills. In many schools and districts, they also include essential questions and required assessments. As schools have become more engaged in the mapping process, these elements have also expanded. There are some schools that have also included some suggested activities and resources. In small schools where there may be only one section of a course or subject, the individual map becomes the consensus map. In larger schools and districts, the consensus map serves as the school's or district's required curriculum. It becomes an invaluable tool used to ensure a consistent curriculum across the grades and subject in a school or district. The maps represent what Robert Marzano, a senior fellow at Mid-Continent Research for Education and Learning (MCREL) and a noted author in student achievement, refers to as the "guaranteed viable curriculum for all children." While the maps represent the agreed-upon curriculum to be taught, teachers have the freedom to incorporate activities and strategies they feel will best meet their students' needs.

Consensus maps are wonderful communication tools with parents, community members, and technical and post-secondary institutions. In addition, they take the place of the old curriculum guide and become the dynamic curriculum framework for your school or district. They are a step into the future and a far cry from handing a new teacher a set of textbooks followed by the words, "Go teach…."

There are two basic approaches to reaching consensus.

1. Using Individual Maps

In this method, you can organize grade level or course teachers together to develop a subject- or course-essential map by identifying

- common essential questions.
- the core content.
- benchmark and critical skills.
- school or districtwide assessments.

2. Revising and Reacting to an Existing Guideline

In this method, you pull together grade-level teachers, course teachers, or mixed groups to

- Review an agreed-upon district or school guideline.
- Review and target state standards.
- Translate the guideline or standards into a mapping format.
- Work in the individual classroom to see how the consensus map plays out in real practice.
- Revisit the first draft of the consensus map and revise it to an active essential map.

Purpose and Primary Focus

Module 7 clarifies the definition of consensus maps. It provides examples and information that will help workshop participants gain a better understanding of consensus maps. Also included in the module are strategies that can help schools or districts with developing consensus maps. Important questions that will serve as a focus for this module include: What is a consensus map? When is a consensus map in the best interest of children? Jacobs (2004) asks us to consider the tension between two questions: Where is consistency critical for learners? Where is flexibility equally as important?

Activities and Supporting Materials

Activities and supporting materials included in this module are intended to help participants clarify the meaning of consensus maps by considering the functions and uses, format and structure, connections with other standards and initiatives, and design strategies and processes. One of the activities in this module focuses on the use of quality filters. As one school developed its maps, it pulled samples from other states and schools. It also pulled the national and statewide standards from other states. These samples are particularly helpful when developing consensus maps. They allow participants to cross-check developing maps for precise language, critical skills, and gaps and repetitions. Many schools and districts also use post-secondary standards as a filter to ensure rigor in their curriculum. These filters combined with the Coaching Protocols in Module 5 can be valuable tools to help ensure high-quality maps.

Training Tips

Ideally, a school or district is able to focus on individual maps first, and then map the actual taught curriculum. Once a read through is conducted, the data can be used to revise the maps and strengthen the curriculum by addressing gaps, repetitions, etc. At that stage, a school and or district may be ready to proceed with consensus maps.

Some schools elect to start with consensus mapping first and then move to individual maps. Unfortunately, outside pressures can be a contributing factor to rushing the process. Sometimes because of schools' performance on mandated assessments, they feel compelled to start with consensus maps to address major gaps or inconsistencies in what is taught across the grades and subjects. In schools with little or no curriculum anchors, starting with consensus maps can be very effective.

Decisions regarding what is included in consensus maps should not be made in isolation. As mentioned earlier, the use of external lenses or filters such as state and national standards need to be used to ensure that the consensus maps reflect best practices, 21st century curriculum, high standards, and higher order thinking. The use of bi-level analysis during the development of the maps can help to ensure a strong core content in the academic area as well as a critical content in 21st century skill areas such as literacy and technology.

The development of consensus maps can be an opportunity to ensure a guaranteed viable curriculum for all students that reflects skills critical for the 21st century.

Online Materials

To use this module, you'll need to access the following online documents:

Module 7, Figure 1: 1st Grade Spanish Consensus Map

Module 7, Figure 2: 5th Grade Math Consensus Map

Module 7, Figure 3: 8th Grade Language Arts Consensus Map

Module 7, Figure 4: 9th Grade Algebra Beginning Map

Module 7, Figure 5: 10th Grade Biology Consensus Map

Module 7, Figure 6: 10th Grade Math Consensus Map

Module 7, Figure 7: 10th Grade Science Consensus Map

Module 7, Figure 8: 12th Grade Writing Consensus Map

Module 7, Figure 9: Middle School Art Consensus Map

Module 7, Figure 10: Fitness Consensus Map

ESSENTIAL QUESTIONS
- When is consensus in the best interest of the students?
- What are consensus maps?

CONTENT
Concept: A consensus map reflects the policy agreed on by a staff that targets those nonnegotiables in each discipline that are to be addressed with consistency and flexibility in a school or district.

- Definition of a Consensus Map
- Functions and Uses
- Sample Consensus Maps: The Components
- Format and Structure
- The Unique Properties of the Subjects
- Connections to State and National Standards
- The Infusion of Bi-Level Thinking
- Design Strategies and Processes
- **TERMS** Bi-Level Thinking, Consensus Maps, Core Maps, Essential Maps, Quality Lenses

SKILLS
- Explain the definition, functions, and possible uses of consensus maps.
- Analyze sample consensus maps for components, structure, and format.
- Identify the unique properties of different subjects.
- Explain where and how local, state, and national standards are integrated into the maps.
- Use documents from the sample quality lenses as filters to cross-check your maps for gaps and articulation of skill.
- Explain where and how bi-level thinking fits in a consensus map.
- Identify different strategies and/or processes that could be used to develop consensus maps.

EVIDENCE OF LEARNING
- Summary notes from the activity... what is a consensus map?
- Key points shared in the large group after reviewing sample consensus maps.
- Summary of unique properties of the subjects.
- Strategies and processes for developing consensus maps.

ACTIVITIES

What Is a Consensus Map? (workshop and discussion)
- Read Chapter 3 (pages 23–28) in *Getting Results with Curriculum Mapping*.
- Discuss the definition of consensus maps, functions and uses, and cautions regarding consensus maps.

Examining Consensus Maps (small group activity)
- At your tables, examine sample consensus maps provided in this training module.
- As a team, identify the common elements.
- Discuss format and structure. Which format would work best in your school or district?
- Discuss the connection with local, state, and national standards. Where do they fit?
- What is the role of bi-level skills in consensus maps?
- What other lenses could be used to ensure high-quality maps?

Unique Properties of Subjects (jigsaw activity)
- Jigsaw pages 29–35 in *Getting Results with Curriculum Mapping*.
- After reading your section, divide into small groups with participants who have read the other sections.
- In your group discuss the key points to consider when wrestling with consensus and flexibility in regards to different disciplines.
- Share key points in the large group.

Design Strategies and Processes (team activity)
- In your school or district team, discuss different strategies and processes that could be used to develop consensus maps. Think creatively. How might you be able to adjust the process to address potential obstacles such as schedules, time, buy-in, etc.?
- Which process do you feel would work best for your school or district?

ASSIGNMENTS

- Take one of your schoolwide assessments in your curricular area, and using the map as a lens, check for the alignment between the skills and content on the map and the assessment. Note any discrepancies, and bring them to the next meeting.
- Select a data report you currently have access to in your curricular area. Use the content and skills on your map to check for alignment with the skills and content on the report. Are these changes or adjustments that could be made in the report that would provide you with better data so you can make better informed instructional decisions? Bring this information to the next training session.

RESOURCES

Hale, J. (2007). *A Guide to Curriculum Mapping*. Thousand Oaks, CA: Corwin Press. Chapter 6.

Jacobs, H.H. (1997). *Mapping the Big Picture: Integrating Curriculum and Assessment K–12*. Alexandria, VA: ASCD. Chapter 4.

Jacobs, H.H. (2004). *Getting Results with Curriculum Mapping*. Alexandria, VA: ASCD. Chapters 2 and 9.

Jacobs, H.H. (2007). Resources on Web site—www.curriculumdesigners.com

Jacobs, H.H. (2007). *Active Literacy Across the Curriculum*. Larchmont, NY: Eye on Education. Chapters 1–9.

Jacobs, H.H. (in press). *Curriculum 21: Essential Education for a Changing World*. Alexandria, VA: ASCD. Chapters 2, 4, and 5.

McTighe, J., and Wiggins, G. (2005). *Understanding by Design*. Alexandria, VA: ASCD. Chapters 1–7.

Udelhofen, S. (2005). *Keys to Curriculum Mapping: Strategies and Tools to Make It Work*. Thousand Oaks, CA: Corwin Press. Chapter 4.

III.

Maintaining, Sustaining, and Integrating
THE SYSTEM

Merging Assessment Data into Maps

Those of us who have taught in the classroom have probably experienced teaching a concept we believed to be important, giving some type of assessment, and grading it only to find out that it didn't provide us with the information we needed to determine if the students really understood the concept. It might have been an engaging assessment for our learners, but the fact was it did not connect or align to what was actually being taught in the classroom. Therefore, the data generated from the assessment didn't help us when it came to making instructional decisions.

How many students were proficient? What were the deficits in student learning? What skills do I need to reteach and to whom? These are just a few of the basic questions teachers encounter after every lesson they teach. As we think about assessments and the important role they play in instruction, we need to consider too, the role that different types of assessments play in providing the data needed to make instructional decisions. It is important to clearly understand which assessments provide a broader picture of learning in the system and which can give you very specific information about the skills needed to address the deficit areas in learning.

As we get further into the mapping process and examine the alignment between critical aspects in the system (e.g., curriculum, assessment, instruction, and professional development), we find that the maps provide the visual picture needed for analysis and the process becomes the vehicle for the thoughtful dialogue needed to calibrate the impact on student learning. The maps can provide the missing link when it comes to clearly "seeing" the alignment between the curriculum and the assessments. They can help us avoid the aforementioned scenario and, instead, provide us with data that we can actually use.

If we consider the assessment data to be the basis for diagnosis and the maps to be the prescription, it further underscores the importance of alignment between the curriculum and the assessments. In order to use the data for making instructional decisions, it has to be detailed enough for us to pinpoint the problem. If we know through analyzing the assessment data that a student is having difficulty reading because the scores in the fluency section of the assessment are low, we can go back to the map and determine when or if fluency is taught, what specific skills are taught, and even look at the types of activities the teacher is using to teach it. We can thus use the data on the maps to prescribe possible changes that can be made in the instructional plan to help the child be successful. This becomes the point when we can start to merge assessment data into the maps.

Three school leaders who had the courage to think about assessment differently are Richard S. Dunlap Jr., principal at West Chester East High School, Jeanne Tribuzzi, director of English Language Arts, and her colleague, Brandon Wiley, director of Staff Development, at West Seneca School District. Their work represents two different approaches to using maps to strengthen their assessments and reporting tools to sharpen the focus on instruction. Their case studies appear in *Using Curriculum Mapping and Assessment Data to Improve Student Learning* by Bena Kallick and Jeff Colosimo.

All of these points will be addressed further in this module as we think about the important role assessment plays in systemic change and how the maps can be used as a tool to be more prescriptive in the instructional process. Mapping has always been predicated on viewing the path for each K–12 student year to year. The analysis of the maps has "big picture" implications for sealing the gaps in student performance. The findings can be used to inform and revise both individual and consensus maps.

Purpose and Primary Focus

Module 8 focuses on assessments and the importance of the alignment of the assessments and the actual taught curriculum reflected in the curriculum maps. Key questions that will serve to focus discussions include: How can we "unpack" assessment data and merge findings into the maps? How can we sustain improvement in student performance? How can the data be used to inform and strengthen individual and consensus maps?

Activities and Supporting Materials

Activities are included to help teams identify the different types of data they have available in their school or district to help them make meaningful instructional decisions to analyze the data, to determine targets for growth, and to use the findings to inform instruction. Participants also have opportunities to check the alignment of the data with the content and skills included in the maps. This process shows teachers how, by tightening the alignment, they can generate better data that can have a greater impact on student performance. We have provided a couple of sample benchmark reports and district maps for schools who may not have immediate access to reports.

Built into the activities is also an opportunity for participants to become more familiar with the software they are using to manage the mapping and assessment data. Workshop participants have a chance to examine reports and determine those that will be more helpful in providing feedback to inform classroom instruction. After discussing different types of assessments, alignment with the maps, and reports that can be generated in the software, teams have a chance to analyze their current assessment system in their school or district and identify changes that if made could provide them with better data that could be used to make instructional decisions in their system.

Training Tips

When designing this module, we assume that your school or district is using a software package to manage the curriculum mapping process and that you have access to achievement reports. If this is not the case, the activities can be modified accordingly. If you are unable to generate electronic reports, you probably have access to state assessment reports or classroom data that can be used for the data analysis activity. Participants should be encouraged to bring some type of data so they can examine the alignment between the assessments and content and skills in their own curriculum. This will make the activities more valuable and provide teachers with data they can use immediately in their own classrooms. One of the most important points made in this module is that alignment between the curriculum and achievement data is critical if it is to be used to maximize the impact on student achievement.

Online Materials

To use this module, you'll need to access the following online documents:

Module 8, Figure 1, Part 1: 7th Grade Math Benchmarks

Module 8, Figure 1, Part 2: 7th Grade Math Curriculum Framework

Module 8, Figure 2, Part 1: 3rd Grade Reading Performance Data

Module 8, Figure 2, Part 2: 3rd Grade Reading Framework

ESSENTIAL QUESTIONS

- How can we "unpack" assessment data and merge findings into the maps?
- How can we sustain improvement in student performance?

CONTENT

Concept: Assessment data is the basis for diagnosis and the maps are the prescription.

- The Array of Assessment Data
- Demographic Data about Students and Staff
- Alignment with Consensus Maps
- Roles of Benchmark Assessments on Consensus Maps
- The Generation of Reports Using Mapping Software
- Gap and Item Analysis Methodologies
- Alignment to the Assessment System
- Alignment to the Reporting Tools
- **TERMS** Assessment Types, Benchmark Reports, Gap and Item Analysis

SKILLS

- Brainstorm the different types of data that are available.
- Identify the types of data that are most helpful in making instructional decisions.
- Check the alignment of the assessments with the content and skills in your consensus maps.
- Determine the role of benchmark assessments in the instructional process.
- Review sample reports that can be generated from the software and determine their uses in making instructional decisions.
- Use the reports to practice gap and item analysis.
- Assess the status of your assessment system and reporting tools and recommend needed changes.

EVIDENCE OF LEARNING

- List of different types of data that can be used to inform instruction
- Feedback from exercise on aligning school or districtwide assessments to the consensus maps
- Uses of software reports in making instructional decisions
- Key points from exercise on using reports to determine gap and item analysis
- Draft assessment plan and recommend changes

ACTIVITIES

Data, Data...Different Kinds of Data (large group and small group discussion)

- In a large group session, brainstorm the different types of data that can help inform instructional decisions.
- Once you have a list, determine the different categories that emerge.
- Discuss at your tables which types of data are most helpful.

Aligning the Data to the Maps (exercise)

- Using the sample data and maps provided in the training module, check the alignment with the maps.
- Are the skills in the assessments the same as the ones listed on the maps? If not, discuss what changes could be made to sharpen the alignment.
- Report your findings in the large group.

Benchmark Assessments (team and small group discussion/activity)

- Read Chapter 9 in *Getting Results with Curriculum Mapping* and refer to the chapters on benchmark assessments in *Using Curriculum Mapping and Assessment Data to Improve Learning*. Discuss the role benchmark assessments play in the instructional process.
- Discuss how the data from these assessments could be used to inform instruction.
- Consider the assessments currently given in your school or district. Do they provide teachers with the data they need to make good instructional decisions? Focus on one specific curricular area, and list the current benchmark assessments you have in place in your school or district.
- Are there changes you would recommend that would strengthen the assessments? (Consider alignment to the consensus maps, when they are given, access to data and reports, etc.)
- Share your example with other members at your table.

Using Reports to Determine Gap and Item Analysis (group discussion and individual team activity)

- Using assessment reports from your school or district, discuss in your table groups how the reports could be used to inform classroom decisions.
- What additional information may be needed?
- Share your thoughts in the larger group.
- Now as an individual team, use one of your reports to check alignment between the skills on the maps and the skills being assessed. What's missing? What changes could you make that would strengthen the alignment?

School or District Assessment Plan (graphic organizer exercise)

- As a team, develop a matrix on chart paper that reflects the assessments at each grade level. (Include four columns.)
- First, identify specific assessments for each curricular area and write them in the first column.
- Following each assessment, write the type of assessment in the second column.
- In the third column, list the types of information that you can glean from each assessment.
- Discuss how it is used to improve instruction...or is it? Review the assessments for balance, alignment to maps, etc.
- What changes would you recommend to strengthen the district or school plan and provide a complete picture of learning? Record your suggestions in the fourth column on the chart paper.
- Report in the large group and process next steps.

ASSIGNMENTS

- In preparation for the next training session, read Chapters 1 and 7 in *Active Literacy Across the Curriculum*.
- Review one of your maps to determine where you might be able to integrate literacy skills in your map. Bring this map to the next training session.

RESOURCES

Costa, A., and Kallick, B. (2007). *Assessing and Reporting Habits of Mind*. Alexandria, VA: ASCD.

Hale, J. (2007). *A Guide to Curriculum Mapping*. Thousand Oaks, CA: Corwin Press.

Jacobs, H.H. (1997). *Mapping the Big Picture: Integrating Curriculum and Assessment K–12*. Alexandria, VA: ASCD. Chapter 5.

Jacobs, H.H. (2004). *Getting Results with Curriculum Mapping*. Alexandria, VA: ASCD. Chapters 7 and 9.

Jacobs, H.H. (2007). Resources on Web site—www.curriculumdesigners.com

Jacobs, H.H. (2007). *Active Literacy Across the Curriculum*. Larchmont, NY: Eye on Education.

Jacobs, H.H. (in press). *Curriculum 21: Essential Education for a Changing World*. Alexandria, VA: ASCD.

Kallick, B., and Colosimo, J. (2008). *Using Curriculum Mapping and Assessment Data to Improve Learning*. Thousand Oaks, CA: Corwin Press.

Martin-Kniep, G. (2007). *Communities that Learn, Lead, and Last: Building and Sustaining Educational Expertise*. John Wiley and Sons, San Francisco, CA. Chapters 4, 5, and 6.

McTighe, J., and Wiggins, G. (2005). *Understanding by Design*. Alexandria, VA: ASCD. Chapter 7.

Udelhofen, S. (2005). *Keys to Curriculum Mapping: Strategies and Tools to Make It Work*. Thousand Oaks, CA: Corwin Press. Chapter 4.

Integrating Literacy Strategies into Maps

What are literacy skills? Who should be teaching them? Many people feel it is the role of language arts teachers. But in truth, all staff must accept ownership in the process if we are going to help students gain the level of proficiency needed to be successful in all aspects of the curriculum. All teachers are language teachers given that the basis of student performance and communication is the individual learner's language capacity.

A few years ago, as a school was working to integrate literacy skills throughout its curriculum, a social studies teacher pulled Ann aside and said, "I will be glad to help teach literacy skills in my courses, but I need help in knowing which ones are most important, and then I need suggestions of possible strategies to incorporate in my teaching." He went on to say that he understood the importance of the skills, but because language arts wasn't his area of expertise, he lacked confidence in knowing what to do and how to do it. Frequently, we hear the same thing from teachers across the country. There is a willingness to help, but they just want to know what skills to teach and how to weave the teaching of literacy skills into their curriculum. Schools that have embarked on this journey have found that the maps provide the cornerstone for this work. When teachers work together to integrate literacy skills in the maps, these maps provide a clear focus for the teachers who may lack the confidence in knowing what to teach. Coupled with professional development on specific literacy strategies and activities in the content areas, the maps provide the momentum for a concerted effort school wide.

Curriculum mapping is a powerful vehicle for directly integrating active literacy across the curriculum to ensure that all teachers are teaching and reinforcing the critical strategies in reading, writing, speaking, and listening so every student has the language capacity he or she needs to be a successful learner. Mapping provides an opportunity for these critical skills to be clearly articulated and mapped across the school. Heidi advocates the following strategies to consider when mapping literacy (Jacobs, 2007):

- Revising and expanding the role of every teacher to an active literacy teacher
- Separating vocabulary into three distinctive types in every classroom
- Integrating creative note taking strategies
- Designating and employing consistent editing and revising of the framework
- Using a formal approach to speaking skills through four discussion types that are assessable
- Technical instruction in speaking in every classroom
- Using curriculum mapping as a unifying schoolwide vehicle to develop formal benchmark assessments

We will touch on them in this module; however, they can be explored in more depth in Heidi's book, *Active Literacy Across the Curriculum.*

We respect and admire the work of the many outstanding researchers in the field of literacy and encourage you to integrate their work directly into the ongoing curriculum. Given the increase and range of English language learners in our schools, the type of strategies used matters greatly. A best practice is to work with your reading specialists to employ those programs and techniques that they find work well with your specific student population. We have provided an extensive list of authors in the resource section of the professional development map of this module.

Purpose and Primary Focus

The primary purpose of Module 9 is to show leaders and leadership teams how mapping can serve as a vehicle to integrate critical cross-curricular skills such as literacy in the schoolwide curriculum.

Several key questions can provide focus for the discussion on the integration of literacy: Why map literacy? How can mapping serve as a tool to integrate literacy skills throughout the curriculum? and How can mapping serve as a unifying vehicle in schools or districts to ensure the teaching of active literacy in every subject at every grade level?

Activities and Supporting Materials

The activities included in Module 9 provide an opportunity for participants to explore the concept of every teacher as an active literacy teacher; key strategies that provide a clear focus on the critical skills in reading, writing, speaking, and listening; and strategies that can be used to integrate literacy skills in the mapping process.

Workshop participants will have an opportunity to learn in more depth about the seven essential literacy strategies that Heidi shares in her book, *Active Literacy Across the Curriculum*. These strategies provide a foundation for clearly integrating literacy skills in maps schoolwide. Participants will also have an opportunity to use sample maps to practice integrating literacy skills in different curricular areas. In addition to the activities included in this module, more specific activities and strategies are included in the book.

Training Tips

As mentioned previously, sometimes the integration of skills like literacy cause a sense of anxiousness by staff who may not have a strong background in this the area. For that reason, all staff should work in a collaborative fashion and be given opportunities for teachers to suggest what training they may need to be successful at teaching them. We have found that concrete examples are extremely helpful to staff who are concerned about time issues. When they see that the teaching of literacy skills can be integrated with their current teaching, it helps to minimize the stress level.

Mapping can help sustain the teaching of literacy across the curriculum. Think about it. If it can work for literacy, it can work for other critical 21st century skills.

Online Materials

To use this module, you'll need to access the following online document:
Module 9, Figure 1: Understanding Weather

ESSENTIAL QUESTIONS

- Why map literacy?
- How can mapping serve as a tool to integrate literacy skills throughout the curriculum?
- How can mapping serve as a unifying vehicle in schools and districts to ensure the teaching of active literacy in every subject at every grade level?

CONTENT

Concept: Teachers from every discipline can use curriculum mapping as a unifying schoolwide vehicle to develop formal benchmark assessments to ensure active literacy in every subject at every grade level.

- Seven Essential Strategies for Integrating Active Literacy in the Curriculum:
    1. Every Teacher is an Active Literacy Teacher
    2. Three Distinctive Types of Vocabulary
    3. Creative Note Taking Strategies
    4. Editing and Revising Framework
    5. Speaking and Listening in Groups
    6. Technical Instruction in Each Classroom
    7. Mapping: A Vehicle to Integrate Formal Benchmark Assessments in Literacy
- Mapping Active Literacy
- **TERMS** Active Literacy, Seven Essential Strategies for Integrating Active Literacy

SKILLS

- Summarize how mapping can serve as a tool to strengthen the teaching of literacy in all subjects at all grade levels by using the Seven Essential Strategies for Integrating Active Literacy.
- Explain why every teacher should be an active literacy teacher.
- Describe where distinctive types of vocabulary could be integrated into maps.
- Determine how mapping could resolve note taking issues.
- Explain how mapping could be used as a tool to ensure a consistent framework for teaching editing and revising.
- Identify types of group speaking and listening skills that could be integrated in the maps.
- Explain how technical listening and speaking skills could be taught throughout the curriculum.
- Explain how mapping can be used as a vehicle to develop formal assessments for active literacy in every subject at every grade level.

EVIDENCE OF LEARNING

- Reasons why every teacher should be an active literacy teacher
- Summary of the Seven Essential Strategies
- Summary of how mapping can serve as a tool to strengthen the teaching of literacy in all grades and subjects
- Coaching strategy ideas for integrating active literacy in maps

ACTIVITIES

Every Teacher an Active Literacy Teacher (workshop)

- Read and discuss the information in Chapter 1 in *Active Literacy Across the Curriculum*. Consider the following questions: What is meant by, "Every teacher should be an active literacy teacher?" What would be the potential benefits and reasons to embrace this philosophy?
- Open the discussion to the larger group.

Seven Essential Strategies (small group exercise)

- Begin by having the entire group read pages 3–13 in *Active Literacy Across the Curriculum*.
- Then, assign table groups one of the following chapters:
  - Integrating Distinctive Types of Vocabulary (pages 17–35)
  - Creative Note Taking (pages 39–57)
  - Editing and Revising (pages 59–79)
  - Speaking and Listening in Groups (pages 79–92)
  - Giving Voice Lessons in Every Classroom (pages 95–109)
- You may opt to have the tables break the chapters down further at their individual tables depending on the amount of time you have for this activity.
- Identify the key points in each section.
- Then, ask each group to identify possible strategies for implementing their area of focus in the maps.
- Summarize your information on chart paper and share your ideas with the entire group.
- Discuss how mapping could serve as a tool to ensure the teaching of active literacy in every grade and subject across the curriculum.

Integrating Active Literacy (small group exercise)

- Using the sample maps provided in Module 1, select one and identify places where you could integrate active literacy strategies in the map.
- Share your revised map with two other colleagues at your table.
- Identify possible coaching strategies you could use to help your colleagues back in your school or district integrate active literacy in their maps.
- Share coaching strategy ideas in the larger group.

ASSIGNMENTS

- Brainstorm individually or in small groups how mapping can be embedded in other professional development in the district. Bring this list to the next session.
- Bring a list of inservices trainings or chunks of time that could be used for curriculum mapping to the next meeting.
- Brainstorm a list of trainings that will be needed by the leaders and staff in the school or district to successfully implement curriculum mapping. Bring this list to the next training session.

RESOURCES

Benjamin, A. (2005). *Writing in the Content Areas*. Larchmont, NY: Eye on Education.

Billmeyer, R. (2007). *Strategies to Engage the Mind of the Learner: Building Strategic Learners*. Omaha, NE: Rachel and Associates.

Jacobs, H.H. (2007). *Active Literacy Across the Curriculum*. Larchmont, NY: Eye on Education. Chapters 1–9.

Jacobs, H.H. (in press). *Curriculum 21: Essential Education for a Changing World*. Alexandria, VA: ASCD.

Martin-Kniep, G. (2007). *Communities that Learn, Lead ,and Last: Building and Sustaining Educational Expertise*. San Francisco: John Wiley and Son. Chapters 4, 5, and 6.

Strong, R.W., Perini, M.J., Silver, H.F., and Tuculescu, G.M., (2002). *Reading for Academic Success*. Thousand Oaks, CA: Corwin Press.

Tomlinson, C.A. (1999). *The Differentiated Classroom*. Alexandria, VA: ASCD.

Developing a Professional Development/ Implementation Plan

Schools that have been successful at integrating curriculum mapping over the long term have done so by making it a part of their culture. It becomes a way of doing business. As educators, we all know that initiatives come and go. What is different about curriculum mapping? Heidi talks about the importance of thinking about mapping systemically in her book, *Getting Results with Curriculum Mapping*. She suggests that you think of mapping as the center of a wheel that holds the spokes together and allows forward movement. A thoughtfully crafted implementation plan can serve as the grounding force needed to make mapping a reality.

The use of an implementation map is an extension of the curriculum mapping process and is a tool that can be helpful in developing a long-term plan. By using the curriculum mapping format, a school or district can lay out their mapping plan for the year. A professional development/implementation map includes your mapping goals for the year, the time devoted to training, essential questions to focus and frame each training session, the concept and content to be taught during each training session, the skills you want the participants to be able to demonstrate as a result of the training, evidence of learning assessment(s), and the assignment to be completed before the next session. This manual is designed so that your team can take the professional development maps that have been included in the modules and adapt them for your school or district.

This professional development tool was designed to help staffs think through the training needed to ensure successful implementation of the mapping process. Schools have used this tool not only to develop schoolwide or districtwide plans, but also to develop individual building plans and plans for study group sessions. Like a curriculum map, the tool keeps you focused on critical questions such as: Why are we teaching this concept? How will teaching it help staff be successful in developing their own quality maps and using the mapping process to make good instructional decisions? The tool also helps a school or district to zero in on the end product or results and think through the training your staff will need to be successful at reaching those goals.

Schools that have sustained change and taken curriculum mapping to another level have developed school or district professional development/implementation plans and then had individual buildings customize plans to reflect the needs of their staff. This allows buildings to work toward a common set of goals but differentiate the training depending on the skill level in their building. Schools have also found it helpful to integrate curriculum mapping training with other initiatives as they are introduced into the school or district. One school was working on implementing reading strategies across the curriculum. As they were developing their implementation map, they found that by having staff bring their curriculum maps to the training session they could better align the appropriate reading strategies with the curriculum that was being taught during that month or unit. Thus, they were able to integrate mapping into all of their training.

In many schools or districts, the school leaders enter the implementation map in the software systems for their leadership teams. This allows them to continually modify and update the map following each training session based on feedback from the staff. It also allows the leaders to experience the entry process. Most schools also have personal and individualized professional expectations. We highly recommend that teachers translate their professional goals to a personal map.

Schools or districts who have used this tool with all of their professional development have found that it helps their staff see how curriculum mapping really is the connector or hub for school improvement. They have also found that they are more efficient and that the valuable time they have for training is better utilized because there is a strong focus. By mapping your school's or district's professional development plan, you are modeling for your staff one of the advanced applications of curriculum mapping.

Purpose and Primary Focus

Module 10 focuses on the professional development/implementation map: a definition, the components, and coaching strategies for developing an implementation map; and benefits.

Guiding questions for this module include: Why map professional development? How can the mapping process be used to increase the quality of professional development in your school or district? and What are the optimum conditions to sustain your mapping work? During this workshop, participants have an opportunity to use the information and develop a draft professional development/implementation map for their school or district.

Activities and Supporting Materials

The activities in Module 10 were designed to coach workshop participants through the development process of designing their own professional development/implementation map. Sample maps from other schools have been provided online for your reference. You will note that some of the templates differ and some are at a starting point or unfinished, but all reflect how the map can be used in a more systemic way. Some schools have started by mapping just the content and skills to get started and then added the other components. Other schools have started right out to map all components included on the template. Whether you use the actual implementation map template or not, the thought process is the same. You begin with the end in mind.

Training Tips

This process can be used by school or district leadership teams. Schools that have been successful in sustaining mapping over the long term have taken the time to develop a road map for implementation.

This process can also help you think through the support structure and the training that teacher/administrator leaders will need to help facilitate the process across the school. Schools that have used implementation maps have found that they are more focused and better utilize the precious time they have for training.

Categories in this professional development/implementation map may be added or adjusted. Some schools find the category entitled "materials" particularly helpful because it pushes them to think through what handouts or supporting materials they will need for that training session. A week prior to the training, they revisit the plan and use it as a tool to keep them focused and ensure that have all the needed materials and equipment for a successful training session.

Schools that use external consultants to help them in the process of developing a professional development and implementation map have found the advice of these individuals to be extremely helpful because they have a better indication where they will be in the process and what specific training will be needed on those days.

Online Materials

To use this module, you'll need to access the following online documents:

Module 10, Figure 1: Implementation Map (Template 1)

Module 10, Figure 2: Implementation Map (Template 2 and Samples)

Module 10, Figure 3: PD Sample Plan

Module 10, Figure 4: Sample Study Group Map

Module 10, Figure 5: Individual PD Map

Module 10, Figure 6: CM Goals Planning Tool

Module 10, Figure 7: PD Building Goal Plan

Module 10, Figure 8: CM Training Session Evaluation Form

ESSENTIAL QUESTIONS
- Why map professional development?
- How can the mapping process be used to increase the quality of professional development in your school or district?
- What are the optimum conditions to sustain your mapping work?

CONTENT

Concept: A professional development/implementation map sharpens focus and can help to sustain long-term change.

- Implementing Mapping: Greatest Hopes/Intended Results
- Goal Setting: Short- and Long-Term Goals
- Finding the Time
- Components of the Professional Development/Implementation Map
- Differentiated Training
- Follow-Through Strategies
- Benefits of Mapping Professional Development
- The Implementation Map: Other Applications
- **TERMS** Professional Development Map, Implementation Map, Differentiated Training

SKILLS
- Identify greatest hopes/intended end results for mapping.
- Identify goals for year one and year two.
- "Unpack" the goals and intended results to determine content and skills that need to be taught in the trainings.
- Brainstorm ways to find time for training and support.
- Map the professional development/implementation plan for the year, including: content, skills, and essential questions; evidence of success; assignments; and resources.
- Incorporate differentiated and integrated training opportunities in the plan.
- Design and include engaging activities to practice the desired skills.
- Integrate follow-through strategies in the plan to provide ongoing support.
- Develop a monitoring plan to collect feedback to refine the professional development/implementation plan.
- Summarize the benefits from mapping the professional development.
- Brainstorm other applications of the process that could help ensure successful implementation in your school or district.

EVIDENCE OF LEARNING
- A list of greatest hopes/intended results
- Monitoring/feedback tool(s) for training sessions
- Draft of short- and long-term goals
- Benefits of the professional development/implementation
- Time allotments for professional development
- Differentiated training suggestions map
- Professional development/implementation map including goals, time line, essential questions, content, skills, evidence of learning, activities, assignments, etc.
- Suggestions for follow-through and accountability
- List of other possible applications for the professional development/implementation map

ACTIVITIES

Greatest Hopes/Intended Results (team and small group exercise)

- In teams, identify your greatest hopes/intended results if your school or district were to implement curriculum mapping. What products, processes, etc., would be in place by the end of year one and year two after implementing curriculum mapping?
- Once you have identified your greatest hopes/intended results, unpack them to determine the content and skills that staff would need to know and be able to do to play their part in helping to achieve the goals/intended results.
- Share your draft with others at your table.

Finding the Time (team exercise)

- Revisit the list of chunks of time that were developed in Module 3. Be sure to include all possible times that could be used for training. (i.e., inservices trainings, faculty meetings.).
- As a team, identify those that would best work for your school.
- Determine the specific days and total amount of time you will have to spend on curriculum mapping.
- Put the dates in the appropriate place on the professional development/implementation map.

Setting Realistic Goals (team and small group exercise)

- Based on the amount of time you have to devote to the project, identify realistic goals for year one and year two.
- Share your goals with others at your table.

Differentiating the Training (team and small group exercise)

- In your team, consider the goals you have identified for the year. Review the list of content and skills that you generated in the first activity and use it as a starting point to think about the training that would needed to be successful at accomplishing the goal.
- Identify specific staff whose training may need to be modified or differentiated because of their level of understanding or possible leadership role they may be playing.
- Determine possible ways that the training could be adjusted.
- Share your plan with other members at your table.

Develop a Professional Development/Implementation Map (workshop)

- Review the sample professional development maps provided in the materials and use them to identify the critical components that you will want to include in your own map.
- Use the backwards planning strategy to identify essential questions, content, skills, and evidence of learning.
- Generate activities that will help participants practice the skills.
- Identify the assignments to be completed prior to the next session.
- Some schools or districts have also chosen to add other areas such as resources or materials needed for training sessions.
- Use the Coaching Protocols from Module 4 to refine your professional development/implementation map.
- Share your map with others at your table.

Follow-Through Strategies (small and large group discussion)

- In small groups, identify ways to build in accountability and provide follow-through support.
- Discuss how these could be integrated in the maps and shared with staff.
- Share ideas in the larger group.

Monitoring the Implementation Process (team and small group exercise)

- Develop a plan to collect feedback from participants following each training sessions that will provide the needed information to refine the next training session. What information would be helpful in assessing the success of the training and determining next steps?
- Consider too, how you could use the evidence of learning to provide helpful feedback as to their level of understanding. Participants' work samples could be used by the training/leadership team to identify what's working and what reteaching may need to occur to move forward.
- Share the plan you have drafted with other members at your table.
- Discuss how this feedback and the implementation map could be used to help you determine your focus and training for year two.

Benefits of a Professional Development/Implementation Map (discussion)

- Discuss benefits and possible uses of a professional development/implementation map.
- What other applications might it have in a school and/or district?

ASSIGNMENTS

- Revisit the Hub exercise that you completed in Module 2. After participating in the other training sessions, are there other initiatives you would add to the list? Have your thoughts changed about how mapping can serve as a linchpin for all initiatives?
- Brainstorm other processes in your school or district. How are they connected to mapping? (e.g., board policies, textbook adoption cycles)? Bring your list to the next training session.

RESOURCES

Hale, J. (2007). *A Guide to Curriculum Mapping.* Thousand Oaks, CA: Corwin Press. Chapter 11.

Jacobs, H.H. (1997). *Mapping the Big Picture: Integrating Curriculum and Assessment K–12.* Alexandria, VA: ASCD.

Jacobs, H.H. (2004). *Getting Results with Curriculum Mapping.* Alexandria, VA: ASCD. Chapters 4 and 10.

Jacobs, H.H. (2007). Resources on Web site—www.curriculumdesigners.com

Jacobs, H.H. (2007). *Active Literacy Across the Curriculum.* Larchmont, NY: Eye on Education.

Jacobs, H.H. (in press). *Curriculum 21: Essential Education for a Changing World.* Alexandria, VA: ASCD.

Joyce, B., and Showers, B. (2002). *Student Achievement through Staff Development.* Alexandria, VA: ASCD. Chapters 4–7.

Martin-Kniep, G. (2007). *Communities that Learn, Lead ,and Last: Building and Sustaining Educational Expertise.* San Francisco: John Wiley and Sons. Chapters 4, 5, and 6.

Udelhofen, S. (2005). *Keys to Curriculum Mapping: Strategies and Tools to Make It Work.* Thousand Oaks, CA: Corwin Press. Chapter 4.

Wiggins, G., and McTighe, J. (2007). *Schooling by Design.* Alexandria, VA: ASCD.

Making the Hub Work: Integrating Initiatives

To "initiate" is to originate, to begin. An initiative tsunami often engulfs our school culture as educators are challenged to fit all new programs in the system. The practical question is, How do we move beyond beginning to sustaining and integrating our well-intended projects? Some schools successfully integrate initiatives into their systems and are able to make lasting changes that dramatically impact the effect on student achievement. Other schools experience fragmentation due to processes or activities occurring in isolation and enter into a juggling act to maintain new initiatives. Feeling overwhelmed or anxious can cause us to lose sight of the purpose and priority. In these schools, we often hear comments like, "Just wait it out; this too shall pass," or "We did that several years ago." These feelings are justified because previous initiatives have not been integrated into the system. Staff perpetuate their feelings of "being done!" instead of seeing mapping as an initiative bringing a value-added component to the system that serves to sharpen the school or district's vision.

How can a school or district introduce mapping so it has a lasting effect on the system? In truth, it is not possible to finalize mapping because knowledge will continue to grow, our learners will continue to change, and the larger world will perpetuate new opportunities. To prepare to map, we need to have a prologue, but there is no epilogue. The work will be ongoing.

An eye-opening exercise for a planning team to consider is to ask teachers, administrators, guidance personnel, media specialists, special educators, and support staff to individually list ALL of the current and upcoming initiatives that require their attention. Almost without exception they will feel overwhelmed, in part, because they find it difficult to see how the various programs are connected. Curriculum mapping software provides a place to go to work this out. Years ago, Heidi called mapping "the electronic town square" of the school community (Jacobs, 2004). For example:

- If a district is committed to integrating its technology programs into the core curriculum, then each teacher can comb through his or her maps and find natural places for integrating specific software or online options for their learners.

- If teachers are engaged in differentiated instruction, they click on their maps and go straight to the lesson plan level. Many software programs actually provide a differentiated instruction tab where teachers directly pull up their class lists and make adjustments within the plans themselves. Even more exciting, the information from those entries will be reflected in report printouts showing any patterns for a specific learner. With this information, teachers can take both the short-term and long-terms view of each child's needs (Tomlinson, 1999).

- If schools wish to become professional learning communities, mapping provides the place for the community to meet and look practically at their work and their students' performance.

- If teachers are working with *Understanding by Design* (2005), the actual unit planning template supported by McTighe and Wiggins can be employed within the mapping software. The concept of "designing backwards" should be an integral part of curriculum mapping choices. In short, Understanding by Design can be operationalized through curriculum mapping.

- If a district is concerned about making Adequate Yearly Progress, then a careful look at the K–12 gaps that need to be addressed and the corresponding standards that need work will be the focus of their mapping reviews.

Purpose and Primary Focus

Module 11 focuses on how mapping can serve as a hub to connect and integrate all initiatives, processes, and applications in the system. Leaders and leadership teams have an opportunity to discover strategies they can use to help staffs in their schools or districts make the connections with curriculum mapping so it becomes the connector for all systems pieces. This can be a powerful tool in aligning all aspects of the system with the vision, thus minimizing fragmentation and intensifying the impact on student achievement. Focus questions include: How can mapping serve as a hub for integrating all initiatives? and How can mapping serve as the connector for all school improvement processes in a school or district?

Activities and Supporting Materials

Activities and supporting materials included in Module 11 focus on the hub effect, making connections, aligning the instructional design process, aligning other processes in the school or district, and suggesting how it can serve as an important tool in communicating with stakeholders.

In the opening activity, participants are asked to think about mapping as a hub or connector and how it might serve as the linchpin for all components in the system. Participants have an opportunity in other activities to visually connect other initiatives and processes in the system with the mapping processes and consider the interrelationship between all the pieces. This leads to the construction of a flowchart that can serve as a communication tool for their staff and stakeholders in their school or district.

Training Tips

There are times during training when facilitators wrestle with taking the time to process information. Take it! The insights gained by staff working through the connections and how each piece supports one another can help strengthen communication and deepen their understanding about systemic change. Improved communication and deeper understanding will help sustain change over the long term.

Online Materials

To use this module, you'll need to access the following online document:

Module 11, Figure 1: Initiatives Graphic Organizer

Module 11, Figure 2: References

ESSENTIAL QUESTIONS

- How can curriculum mapping serve as a hub for integrating all initiatives?
- How can mapping serve as the connector for all school improvement processes in a school or district?

CONTENT

Concept: Mapping becomes an integrating force to address not only curriculum issues, but also programmatic ones.

- The Hub Effect
- Connections, Connections, Connections: Integrating Other School Improvement initiatives (e.g., Habits of Mind, UbD, PLCs, High School Reform)
- Alignment to Instructional Design (e.g., Lesson Plans, Units, Understanding by Design)
- Alignment to Other Processes (e.g., Board Policies, Curriculum Review Process, Textbook Adoption Cycle, Professional Development)
- Mapping: Communicating with Your Stakeholders
- **TERMS** Initiatives, Instructional Design Process, Hub Effect, Lesson Plans, Units

SKILLS

- Explain what is meant by the phrase, "hub effect."
- Connect other initiatives to mapping and discuss how mapping could be embedded in the training of those initiatives.
- Explain the alignment of instructional design to the mapping process.
- Construct an alignment model that connects mapping to other school and district processes.
- Explain how mapping can be used as a communication tool with school and district stakeholders.

EVIDENCE OF LEARNING

- Explanation of the hub effect
- Highlights from the exercise on alignment and instructional design
- Connecting the initiatives: The Next Evolution (Module 2)
- Draft alignment model that connects mapping to other school or district processes
- Strategies for using mapping as a tool to communicate with stakeholders

ACTIVITIES

Mapping as a Hub (discussion)

- Now that you have had a chance to explore mapping in more depth, discuss what is meant by mapping as a hub.
- How has your opinion changed or expanded as you have learned more about mapping?
- How could you help colleagues back in your school and district gain a deeper understanding?

Connecting Mapping to Other Initiatives (small group exercise)

- Revisit the organizer developed in Module 2 on Connecting Initiatives. Are there changes you would make?
- Identify where the initiatives could be integrated in the maps (i.e., Individual, Consensus, and Implementation).

Aligning Mapping and the Instructional Design Process (pair activity)

- Using the sample maps provided in Module 1, select one map and work together to identify possible coaching strategies you could use with colleagues to help them connect the maps with lesson and unit plan design.
- Share your strategies with other members at your table.

Mapping: Connecting All School and/or District Processes (group exercise)

- Brainstorm the other processes that are currently used in your school or district (i.e., curriculum review process, building/ school improvement process, professional development).
- Determine where and how curriculum mapping could be integrated in the process. You may find it helpful to brainstorm the processes in the large group and then break into smaller groups so each small group can focus on one specific area.
- If you break into smaller groups, allow time to have groups share their process and plan for integration.

Mapping: Communicating with Your Stakeholders (team and small group brainstorming session)

- In teams, brainstorm possible ways you could use the maps to communicate with stakeholders in your school or district. Also, consider how you could help stakeholders understand what mapping is and the benefits to a school and district.
- Share your team's suggestions in the larger group.

ASSIGNMENTS

- In preparation for the last training module, conduct a Web search in your curricular area. Look specifically for best practices, future trends, innovations, or changes in the curriculum that might impact instruction. What are the most important "big ideas" that you teach in your curricular area?

RESOURCES

Costa, A., and Kallick, B. (2007). *Integrating and Sustaining Habits of Mind*. Alexandria, VA: ASCD.

Hale, J. (2007). *A Guide to Curriculum Mapping*. Thousand Oaks, CA: Corwin Press.

Jacobs, H.H. (1997). *Mapping the Big Picture: Integrating Curriculum and Assessment K–12*. Alexandria, VA: ASCD.

Jacobs, H.H. (2004). *Getting Results with Curriculum Mapping*. Alexandria, VA: ASCD.

Jacobs, H.H. (2007). Resources on Web site—www.curriculumdesigners.com

Jacobs, H.H. (2007). *Active Literacy Across the Curriculum*. Larchmont, NY: Eye on Education.

Jacobs, H.H. (in press). *Curriculum 21: Essential Education for a Changing World*. Alexandria, VA: ASCD.

Martin-Kniep, G. (2007). *Communities that Learn, Lead, and Last: Building and Sustaining Educational Expertise*. John Wiley and Sons, San Francisco, CA. Chapters 4, 5, and 6.

McTighe, J., and Wiggins, G. (2005). *Understanding by Design*. Alexandria, VA: ASCD.

Tomlinson, C.A. (1999), *The Differentiated Classroom*. Alexandria, VA: ASCD.

Udelhofen, S. (2005). *Keys to Curriculum Mapping: Strategies and Tools to Make It Work*. Thousand Oaks, CA: Corwin Press. Chapter 1.

Advanced
MAPPING TASKS

Into the Future: Updating Maps for the 21st Century Learner

Our learners are always moving into their future. The question is whether we, as educators, are doing all that we can to prepare them. It is hard to stay current on every breakthrough in every field of study. We have our hands full in schools, yet we advise that periodic and regular reviews of maps to update them and to keep our work timely are a critical part of becoming an operational learning community.

Throughout the training, we have tried to show how curriculum mapping can become the hub for all school improvement efforts in a system. Every aspect of the work in the school can emanate from the hub, and the hub serves as an organizing force or connector for bringing together the group of dedicated professionals. Thus, it allows teachers and administrators to become dreamers and confident risk takers in their quest to help all students become independent, lifelong learners.

The systemic process of curriculum mapping serves as the catalyst to

- Develop a dynamic, focused, and articulated curriculum for all students in the school.
- Strengthen the alignment of all aspects of instruction in the system.
- Connect all school improvement initiatives in the school.
- Create a long-term vision for change and implementation plan.
- Develop an implementation plan that integrates the research-based professional development needed to ensure success.

- Integrate a feedback loop that provides data and feedback used to continually sharpen the focus.
- Rethink the support structure and resources needed to ensure lasting change.

This is only the beginning of the journey. The real power of mapping lies in the creative applications that are yet to come. How can mapping help you to prepare your students for an uncertain future?

Advanced curriculum mapping strategies translate into proactive planning to address future needs for your learner. Jacobs (in press) suggests that there are two levels of change for schools to consider—one is short term, "upgrading" practice, and the other is long term by developing "new versions" of schooling.

Jacobs (in press) suggests that teachers take a 21st century pledge to replace at least one dated assessment with a contemporary one. By reading the maps and deliberately making these changes, students not only get the benefit of a new approach but they see their teachers modeling revision. For example, instead of having students carry out an oral report on index cards, students may use a podcast. Instead of having students produce a book report, they create a Web cast. In her view, schools need to decide in which century they are operating.

One of the most exciting new directions is student mapping. We support the linkage between student digital portfolios, as advocated by David Niguidula (2007), and teacher maps. In a pilot program we ran in Lakeville, Minnesota, an innovate teacher, Beth Beckwith, worked with our team to show how we could engage children in entering their portfolio data into the teacher maps. The work showed that the children really did understand how the teacher map was showing the direction of the curriculum and how their work reflected progress. One of the most impressive institutional signs of contemporary thinking is the commitment of the state of Rhode Island. For the first time, a state has asked its learners to become self-accountable by formally requiring that graduates produce their own digital portfolio that corresponds directly to graduation requirements and standards. We see this as student self-navigation.

Strategic Grouping for Professional Reviews

Another improvement that can be addressed at an advanced mapping stage is to rethink the ordinary and dated approach to faculty and administrative grouping. Rather than always meeting by department or by grade level for planning purposes, a different approach would be to ask who should meet together to solve a specific problem. We propose and list strategic grouping patterns to match the nature of a task with the appropriate team:

- **Vertical** (e.g., K–12; extended departmental meetings)
- **Targeted vertical** (e.g., K–1; 3–6; V 7–11; 1–12)
- **Across grade level** (all third grade, all teachers of freshmen)
- **Targeted cross-grade level** (e.g., interdisciplinary 7th grade team)
- **Extended team** (e.g., special area teachers, special ed. staff, ESL)
- **Feeder pattern** (e.g., in larger districts; only those sharing the same students; within school following student groups)
- **Expanded team** (e.g., virtual groupings (online); parents; community; internships; global partners)

Purpose and Primary Focus

Module 12 is designed to encourage leaders and leadership teams to imagine other applications of mapping that will help their schools and districts stay focused on the future needs of your students. By expanding the applications and integrating them system-wide, mapping becomes a "way of doing business" and not just an event. How can mapping serve as a tool to launch curriculum plans for our students' futures? How can the feedback spiral be used in mapping to ensure a curriculum for the 21st century? What other aspects of the system could be strengthened in your school or district by using the maps as a lens to sharpen teaching and learning? and How can mapping serve as a hub for planning future directions with new data? These are just a few of the questions that participants will consider as they continue to shape a new vision for their school or district.

We recommend that this module's professional development map more than any of the others provides the place to go to keep exploring additional possibilities. More schools should promote proactive learning among teachers to search out what is new and to investigate new learning possibilities.

Activities and Supporting Materials

The activities in Module 12 are intended to help leaders and leadership teams move beyond the basics and consider the "what ifs…." They suggest possible starting points to further integrate curriculum mapping into the fabric of the school or district. These activities "zoom in" on a few specific areas in the system and show how mapping can serve as a tool to strengthen the alignment between them, thus providing better data to make informed instructional decisions. By using the maps as a focal point for discussions, schools or districts can use the data from the maps to cross walk between the other aspects of the system to check coherence and alignment.

One of the challenges that schools and districts encounter in the journey is how to keep maps current and how to expand the use of the data they provide to make structural changes in the system. When leaders and leadership teams are able to have these types of discussions, they are able to maximize the benefits of the mapping process.

Training Tips

The ideas in this module are intended to stimulate your thinking about mapping from a systems perspective. It is an opportunity to take an honest look at your system and consider what's not working. What is there that, if changed, could provide an even stronger educational program for the students in your school or district and better prepare them for the 21st century? Activities suggested are not all-inclusive but intended to show you a few possible applications as you continue to explore mapping as a hub for school improvement.

Online Materials

To use this module, you'll need to access the following online document:

Module 12, Figure 1: 9th Grade Film Documentary Curriculum Map

Module 12, Figure 2: Example of Updated Curriculum Map

ESSENTIAL QUESTIONS

- How can mapping serve as a tool to launch curriculum plans for our students' futures?
- How can the feedback spiral be used in mapping to ensure a curriculum for the 21st century?
- How can mapping serve as a hub for planning future directions with new data?

CONTENT

Concept: Curriculum mapping can serve as the link to the future.

- Curriculum for the 21st Century
- Curriculum Mapping: A Link to the Future
- Keeping Maps Current: Reflecting the Future
- The Feedback Spiral: A Component of Continued Learning
- Advanced Applications: Students' Maps, Digital Portfolios, Global Connections
- A Hub for Planning Future Directions
- **TERMS** Global Connections, Portfolios, Student Maps

SKILLS

- Compare and contrast Curriculum for the 21st Century with the current curriculum.
- Identify ways that curriculum mapping can serve as a link to the future.
- Explain how diary mapping, the read through process, and the feedback spiral are keys to sustaining change.
- Identify strategies that can be used to keep maps current.
- Review examples of advanced applications—student maps, digital portfolios, global connections—and determine links/ connections with curriculum mapping.
- Brainstorm expanded uses of the maps in your school or district.
- Expand the hub to reflect the future.

EVIDENCE OF LEARNING

- Key points from the workshop on Curriculum for the 21st Century
- List of ways that curriculum mapping can serve as a link to the future
- Strategies for keeping maps current
- A list of advanced applications for curriculum mapping
- List of expanded uses of mapping
- The hub organizer revised

ACTIVITIES

21st Century Curriculum (workshop)

- Use the information about 21st Century Skills in hyperlinks provided in the resource section as a foundation for the discussion on 21st Century Curriculum.
- In like curricular groups, discuss the implications for your area.
- Use the information that you found on the Web as a filter to affirm or dispute the implications your group generated.
- What are the most important concepts you teach that prepare students for the future?
- What changes would you recommend in your curriculum?

Curriculum Mapping: A Link to the Future (discussion)

- Discuss what is meant by the phrase "Curriculum Mapping: A Link to the Future." How can maps serve as a vehicle to support the teaching of a 21st century curriculum?
- At your tables, generate specific examples or strategies that affirm the phrase and share them in the large group.

Keeping Maps Current (team exercise)

- In teams, brainstorm ways that your school or district could keep the maps current. Consider how the feedback spiral could be used to help sustain your school or district's work in mapping. Factor in the school or district parameters and potential obstacles. Determine which strategies might be the most effective.
- Share your strategies in the larger group.

Advanced Applications: Reflecting the Future (workshop)

- After sharing sample applications (student maps, digital portfolios, global connections, etc.), ask table teams to discuss the implications for instruction. What other possibilities could be explored? How could these and future applications be integrated into the mapping process?
- Share highlights from your discussion in the larger group.

Bringing It Home (individual/team exercise)

- As an individual or team, think about what is working and not working in your district. How might mapping help to address the weaknesses? Brainstorm possible starting points in your school or district to expand the use of the maps and move toward a systems approach. After brainstorming possibilities, identify your top priority.
- Share your thoughts with other participants at your table.

The Hub Revisited (small group discussion)

- In small groups, revisit the other district initiatives and determine where and how mapping can enhance the implementation of those initiatives. (The data you collected in the hub activity in Module 2 can serve as a starting point for this discussion.)
- What changes, additions, and revisions would you suggest now that you have a deeper understanding of the process?

ASSIGNMENTS

- Identify assignments that will help your staff continue to focus on the future as you continue your work in the mapping process.

RESOURCES

Costa, A., and Kallick, B. (1995). *Assessment in the Learning Organization.* Alexandria VA: ASCD. Pages 25–29.

Hyerle, D. (2008). *Visual Tools for Transforming Information into Knowledge.* Thousand Oaks, CA; Corwin Press.

Jacobs, H.H. (1997). *Mapping the Big Picture: Integrating Curriculum and Assessment K–12.* Alexandria, VA: ASCD.

Jacobs, H.H. (2004). *Getting Results with Curriculum Mapping.* Alexandria, VA: ASCD. Chapter 9.

Jacobs, H.H. (2007). Resources on Web site—www.curriculumdesigners.com.

Jacobs, H.H. (in press). *Curriculum 21: Essential Education for a Changing World.* Alexandria, VA: ASCD.

Udelhofen, S. (2005). *Keys to Curriculum Mapping: Strategies and Tools to Make It Work.* Thousand Oaks, CA: Corwin Press. Chapter 4.

Wiggins, G., and McTighe, J. (2007). *Schooling by Design.* Alexandria, VA: ASCD.

www.21stcenturyskills.org

www.skills21.org /the Jason Project

www.jason.org/public/home.aspx

www.richerpicture.com

www.curriculum21.com

Glossary of Mapping Terms

A

Active Literacy: The integration of critical language skills (i.e., listening, speaking, reading, and writing) into the daily curriculum in every class.

Alignment: Agreement or coherence between the essential questions, content, skills, assessments, and standards adopted by the district. Maps allow us to see three types of alignment: internal alignment, external alignment to standards, and cumulative alignment K–12.

Assessments: Demonstrations of learning aligned to the benchmarks and standards that allow students to show you what they know. They are products and performances used as evidence of skill development and content understanding.

Assessment Type: The various kinds of assessments such as quiz, test, performance assessment, essay, etc., that allow students to demonstrate their learning.

B

Benchmarks: Specific developmental statements regarding performance-based standards. Benchmarks are usually defined in behavioral and observable terms.

Big Ideas: Important core concepts, understandings, or theories. Big ideas go beyond discrete skills and focus on larger concepts, processes, or themes.

Bi-Level Analysis: The examination of student work and performance data on two levels—the subject matter concepts and skills, and the requisite language capacity (e.g., linguistic patterns, three types of distinctive vocabulary, and editing and revising strategies).

C

Coaching Protocols: Tools that include the critical criteria for exemplary products. They are used to sharpen focus and ensure quality work.

Concept: A relational statement that provides the focus and basis for acquiring knowledge. It is synonymous with the enduring understanding or big idea.

Consensus/Core Maps: Agreed-upon curriculum identified by teachers and administrators that determines which elements must be consistently taught by all teachers in a course or subject and where flexibility will be critical.

Content: Subject matter, key concepts, facts, topics, and important information.

Curriculum Mapping: A systemic process that can improve student performance by sharpening the alignment of all aspects of the curriculum to reduce repetitions and gaps, and strengthen the articulation of skills.

D

Diary Maps: A map where data are entered on an ongoing basis. Periodically, whether every few weeks or trimester, you will stop and reflect on your work with learners and make an entry.

Differentiated Professional Development: Modified professional development based on the level of understanding of the learners.

Differentiation: The process of modifying or delineating some aspect of instruction: the content, process, product, or learning environment to address the needs of the learners.

E

Enduring Understanding: The important understandings that have lasting value beyond the classroom.

Entry Points: Possible openings or entrances where curriculum mapping can be integrated into the current structure or processes in a school or district. This allows it to become part of the system.

Essential Maps: A revision of agreements that are made by teachers and administrators that determine which elements must be consistently taught by all teachers in the course and where flexibility will be critical.

Essential Questions: Overarching questions provide focus for the unit and are aligned to a key concept.

H

Hub: A connector or linchpin that connects all aspects of the school improvement process.

I

Individual Maps: Maps developed by individual teachers that reflect what they teach in their classes or subjects. They include essential questions, content, skills, and assessments.

Initiatives: Programs, projects, and ideas implemented by schools and districts to improve some aspect of the system.

L

Lessons: Organized instructional plans aligned to assessment targets. The concept of backwards design suggests that you start your design work with the assessment targets and tasks fully described. Once that is accomplished, you design your lessons so that students are fully instructed around the content and skills that will be called for in those assessments. It is a reverse of the model that asks for lesson plans and then later for assessment designs. "Backward design" provides a clear lens for examining your instructional time to make certain that it is purposeful toward benchmarks and standards.

Like-Group Reviews: Read throughs that focus on a specific curricular area. For example, all of the teachers in the language arts department might read through the course maps for their department to look for gaps, repetitions, and the articulation of skills.

M

Map: A visual method for projecting yearly plans as well as monthly plans for the classroom based on a calendar sequence from month to month that describes the scope of what is taught. Maps include essential questions, content, skills, and assessments.

Mixed-Group Reviews: Read throughs of maps that involve teachers from different curricular areas. These types of reviews can help provide a better understanding of the curriculum across the school and district. They can also be used to identify where specific cross-curricular skills or specific school and district goals are included in the curriculum.

N

Nonnegotiables: The core elements that must be taught in the curriculum.

P

Portfolios: A representative collection of a person's work that serves as evidence of understanding.

Power Standards: The most important standards.

Professional/Implementation Development Map: An organizational tool that uses the mapping format to develop a yearlong plan for implementation. It includes training times, essential questions, content to be taught, skills that participants should demonstrate, products or evidence that will be produced during the training, and assignment(s) that participants should complete prior to the next training.

Professional Learning Communities (PLCs): A conceptual model developed by Richard DuFour and his colleagues for transforming schools. It focuses on the following principles: A Shared Mission, Vision, Values, and Goals; Collaborative Teams; Collective Inquiry; Action Orientations and Experimentations; Continuous Improvement; and Results Orientation.

Projected/Projection Map: A map that has been created prior to teaching a course or subject and then revised on an ongoing basis as the school year progresses.

Q

Quality Lenses: Exemplary samples (e.g., maps, standards) from other schools and states that can serve as filters when developing quality consensus maps.

R

Read Through Process: The process following the development of the maps in which the teachers become editors for the maps for the entire building.

S

School-Based Support Structures: Key programmatic structures that have a direct effect on curriculum, assessment, and instruction: schedule (daily, annual, and long-term); grouping of students (within classrooms, throughout the institution, and by class size); and grouping of personnel (into teams, departments, and roles).

Seven Essential Strategies for Integrating Active Literacy: Specific strategies for integrating critical language skills across the curriculum identified by Heidi Hayes Jacobs. The strategies include: revising and expanding the role of all teachers so they incorporate speaking, reading, listening, and writing activities with all learners in all subjects; organizing vocabulary into three distinctive types (high-frequency words, specialized terminology, and embellishing words) with specific instructional approaches in every classroom; developing creative note taking strategies that cause students to extract and react to information; designing and employing a consistent editing and revising framework for writing K–12; assessing formal speaking skills through the use of discussion approaches; employing technical instruction to develop the human voice and body as communication instruments; and using curriculum mapping as the school and districtwide tool for implementing and monitoring the use of these strategies.

Seven-Step Curriculum Mapping Review Process: The process or sequence developed by Heidi Hayes Jacobs for creating and analyzing curriculum maps in a school or district. The steps include: Collecting the Data, The First Read Through, Small Like- and Mixed-Group Review, Large Like- and Mixed-Group Review Comparisons, Determine Immediate Revision Points, Determine Points Requiring Some Research and Planning, and Plan for the Next Review Cycle.

Skills: The targeted proficiencies; technical actions and strategies.

Standards: Statements that reflect the larger outcomes that we expect all students to be able to demonstrate before they leave our school. Most state departments of education have already established standards. Districts often add to those standards based on their local needs.

Student Mapping: Digital portfolios.

T

Targeted Work Groups: Task forces that are organized flexibly to respond to specific emerging needs. When the work of the task force is completed, it is disbanded.

21st Century Skills: Skills students need to be successful in the 21st century. They include: cross-curricular skills and learning to learn skills.

U

Understanding by Design (UbD): A set of ideas and practices that helps you think more purposefully and carefully about the nature of any design that has understanding as its goal. It is based on the work of Jay McTighe and Grant Wiggins and focuses on the principles of "backwards design."

Unit: A curricular unit aligned to standards that encompass some of the major areas of focus in a given developmental period. It includes the essential questions, content and skills that will be addressed, specific lessons that will be used, and assessments that will be required.

Unpacking Standards: Process of clearly defining the critical content and skills embedded in a standard that students need to know and be able to demonstrate to show mastery of the standard.

About the Authors

Heidi Hayes Jacobs is the president of Curriculum Designers, Inc., and she has served as an education consultant to thousands of schools nationally and internationally. She works with schools and districts, K–12, on issues and practices pertaining to curriculum reform, instructional strategies to encourage critical thinking, and strategic planning. Dr. Jacobs has served as an adjunct associate professor in the Department of Curriculum and Teaching at Teachers College, Columbia University, since 1981 and continues to teach there every summer. The fundamental backbone of her experience comes from her years as a teacher of high school, junior high school, and elementary children in Utah, Massachusetts, and New York.

ASCD has published three of her previous books, *Getting Results with Curriculum Mapping, Interdisciplinary Curriculum: Design and Implementation,* and *Mapping the Big Picture: Integrating Curriculum and Assessment K–12.*

Her doctoral work was completed at Columbia University's Teachers College in 1981 where she studied under a national Graduate Leadership Fellowship from the U.S. Office of Education. Her master's degree is from Universtiy of Massachusetts at Amherst and her undergraduate studies were at the University of Utah in her hometown of Salt Lake City. You can contact her at her Web site, www.curriculumdesigners.com, or by e-mail at heidi@ curriculumdesigners.com.

Ann Johnson is an independent consultant and the director of Professional Development for Curriculum Designers, Inc. She works with public, independent, and post secondary institutions nationally and internationally on implementing curriculum and assessment reform, developing high-quality leadership teams, and developing training and implementation plans. Her practical approach to design and alignment is based on her experiences as a classroom teacher, administrator, adjunct professor, and leader in schools that have implemented long-term curriculum alignment and mapping initiatives.

Her extensive work with schools and leadership teams on implementing curriculum and assessment reform, training teachers and administrators in the curriculum and assessment design process, and coaching leadership teams in developing implementation plans is featured in Heidi Hayes Jacob's book, *Getting Results with Curriculum Mapping;* in ASCD's DVD, *Getting Results with Curriculum Mapping;* in *Assessment in a Learning Organization: Shifting the Paradigm* by Art Costa and Bena Kallick; and in a series on curriculum for the *Video Journal of Education.* Ann is also working on a project with ASCD and Dr. Jacobs and serves as a mentor and coach to ASCD faculty members from the Pacific Rim (Japan and Australia) in curriculum mapping.

Ann received her bachelor's degree in speech and theater, her master's in curriculum and instructional design, and her doctorate in educational administration. Her dissertation focused on implementing complex innovations like authentic assessment and curriculum mapping using a comprehensive professional development structure and plan. You can contact Ann by telephone: 515-268-9821, e-mail: ajohnson199@msn.com

Related ASCD Resources

At the time of publication, the following ASCD resources were available; for the most up-to-date information about ASCD resources, go to www.ascd.org. ASCD stock numbers are noted in parentheses.

Networks

Visit the ASCD Web site (www.ascd.org) and search for "networks" for information about professional educators who have formed groups around topics like "Interdisciplinary Curriculum and Instruction." Look in the "Network Directory" for current facilitators' addresses and phone numbers.

Online Courses

Creating Standards-Based Curricula (#PD03OC34)

Print Products

Curriculum Technology Quarterly, Spring 2003: Connecting Curriculum Mapping and Technology (#103310)

Educational Leadership, December 2003/January 2004: New Needs, New Curriculum (#104026)

Mapping the Big Picture: Integrating Curriculum and Assessment K–12 by Heidi Hayes Jacobs (#197135)

THE WHOLE CHILD The Whole Child Initiative helps schools and communities create learning environments that allow students to be healthy, safe, engaged, supported, and challenged. To learn more about other books and resources that relate to the whole child, visit www.wholechildeducation.org.

For more information, visit us on the World Wide Web (http://www.ascd.org), send an e-mail message to member@ascd.org, call the ASCD Service Center (1-800-933-ASCD or 703-578-9600, then press 2), send a fax to 703-575-5400, or write to Information Services, ASCD, 1703 N. Beauregard St., Alexandria, VA 22311-1714 USA.